ISBN: 978-0-692-70209-3 (paperback)
1. Men's Issues

For additional information including orders:
www.thomaspaulmills.com

Scripture taken from the New King James Version® or marked (NKJV). Copyright © 1982 by Thomas Nelson. Used by permission. All rights reserved.

Scripture quotations taken from the New American Standard Bible® or marked (NASB), Copyright © 1960, 1962, 1963, 1968, 1971, 1972, 1973, 1975, 1977, 1995 by The Lockman Foundation. Used by permission. (www.Lockman.org)

Scripture quotations taken from the Holy Bible, New Living Translation or marked (NLT), Copyright © 1996, 2004, 2007, 2013, 2015 by Tyndale House Foundation. Used by permission of Tyndale House Publishers, Inc., Carol Stream, Illinois 60188. All rights reserved.

Scripture quotations from THE MESSAGE or marked (MSG). Copyright © by Eugene H. Peterson 1993, 1994, 1995, 1996, 2000, 2001, 2002. Used by permission of NavPress. All rights reserved. Represented by Tyndale House Publishers, Inc.

Scripture quotations taken from the American King James Version of the Bible or marked (AKJV) are permitted via public domain beginning on November 8, 1999.

Scripture taken from the Common English Bible® or marked (CEB)® Copyright © 2010, 2011 by Common English Bible.™ Used by permission. All rights reserved worldwide.

Scripture taken from THE HOLY BIBLE, NEW INTERNATIONAL VERSION ® NIV® Copyright © 1973, 1978, 1984 by International Bible Society® Used by permission. All rights reserved worldwide.

Author's Note: Some of the characters and events in this book are fictitious. Any similarity to actual persons, living or dead, or actual events is purely coincidental and unintentional. All stories pertaining to Thomas Paul Mills and Ralph K. McLelland are true and factual.

Printed in the United States of America.

"Many men talk about life change, but very few actually experience it. Many men talk about doing something that God has put on their heart, but very few actually do it. *Rubble to Redemption* graciously sheds light on the assault against our heart and what God has provided for us to prevail. I experienced clarity, encouragement and strength through reading this book."

—GARY BARKALOW

FORMERLY WITH RANSOMED HEART MINISTRIES,
AUTHOR OF *IT'S YOUR CALL* AND
FOUNDER OF THE NOBLE HEART MINISTRY

CONTENTS

ACKNOWLEDGEMENTS

THANKS...

To Bruce and Jeanne Edwards. I couldn't ask for a better graphic design team. You made the book look great inside and out.

To my editor, Leslie Wilson for encouraging me to remember the importance of story throughout the book. It was because of this that I delved deeper into my own story and discovered the legacy my father left me.

To Gary Barkalow for pursuing your passion to help others find their own. Your support was so helpful throughout the process of writing this book.

To Janelle Guitelli for your faithful prayers and for praying the words "Rubble to Redemption" that night in our couples group.

To Susie Larson for your encouragement and wisdom.

To my friends and family for all your kind words and prayers. They have helped far more than you will ever know.

To Ralph for showing me what it truly means to experience the fathering of God through the brothering of men. This book would not have happened without your partnership and friendship. Shoulder to shoulder, brother. Here we go.

To Wendy for your steadying and calming words when doubts would creep in. You are a precious gift to me and I'm excited to see what Father God has in store for us in the next chapter of our marriage. I love you.

And finally, to Father God. There will never be enough words to express how much you mean to me. I am so grateful for being invited into this amazing adventure with you. You are the best Dad a man could have. I love you.

AUTHOR'S NOTES

This book is about receiving God's fathering through our brothers as opposed to turning our brothers into fathers.

Brothering is a word that is used in this book to describe the process of receiving God's fathering in human form through our brothers. Some have suggested that I use the word "brotherhood" instead. I assume this is due to the fact that word "brothering" is not listed in most of our dictionaries. Though having a band of brothers (brotherhood) is critical in a man's life, it does not specifically describe the act of bringing God's fathering through our brothers (brothering). Words matter. Language is a powerful tool, but we must allow it to be fluid if we are to develop new ways of bringing meaning to our experiences. This not only involves expanding our own personal vocabulary, but the lexicon itself.

The words, "brother" or "brothers" refer to those we allow to walk with us along the journey whether they are a blood relative or not.

The word, "Father" with a capital "F" refers to God or Jesus. The word, "father" with a small "f" refers to our human fathers.

The Brothering—Interactive Study Questions are just that— interactive. It is preferable that they be done in a group setting with other men.

The Fathering are meditations based on the scriptures presented in their corresponding chapters. These are meant to draw us into the Father's love for us as His sons. Take time to let God father you as you read them and allow others to read them to you.

A Son's Prayer are prayers meant to lead us into a more intimate and vulnerable interaction with Father God. Though not meant as any kind of formula, these prayers are designed to foster more transparency with God about the rubble in our lives and our desperate need for His fathering.

Some of the characters and events in this book are fictitious. Any similarity to actual persons, living or dead, or actual events is purely coincidental and unintentional. All stories pertaining to Thomas Paul Mills and Ralph K. McLelland are true and factual.

FOREWORD

This is a book about vulnerability, so let's get that out of the way right off the bat. I've struggled with walking with God most of my life. It's been a struggle to walk with others as well. My mind is always running like a motor that never shuts off. I get so focused on what's coming next that I end up running up ahead and traveling the journey alone. But then, when I least expect it, something happens—God speaks deep into my heart and I know He's there.

One of those moments occurred in Colorado last year. Colorado has always been a place where God has spoken to me, even during times when I wasn't walking with Him. I was attending a Noble Heart Base Camp gathering at Bear Trap Ranch held by our good friend, Gary Barkalow.

It was during that weekend that God tugged at my heart because of the sharing of one man, Tom Mills. Tom's willingness to be vulnerable opened the door for God to begin a friendship and eventually this ministry—even though we lived 1100 miles apart.

You'll read more about that story a little later. You'll also hear more of his story as well as a few parts of mine. Personal experience expressed in the form of story is the language of the heart. Our individual stories may differ, but the themes and feelings are often the same.

Perhaps I'll hear your story sometime as well and share more of mine so we can both experience this healing process that was designed by our Father.

We all walk along a common journey, a common trail that leads us to our true Father if we are willing to take the risk of being vulnerable with Him.

Ask yourself the following questions:

- Am I willing to remove my mask and be open with God and others?
- Am I willing to be vulnerable like I have never been before?
- Am I willing to be rescued or—more importantly—first admit that I need to be rescued?

Confess your sins one to another so you may be whole and healed, the prayer of a righteous man is a Holy thing.

JAMES 5:16 (NKJV)

God sent His Son to walk the face of this earth so we would understand what it looks like to have a true relationship with

Him as our Father and in doing so understand how to have true relationships with others as well.

Come along with us as we uncover and remove the rubble from our lives. And as we learn the process of being fathered by God through the brothering of men.

Saddle up there boys, it's time to ride.

Ralph K. McLelland

RUBBLE TO REDEMPTION

Experiencing the Fathering of God
Through the Brothering of Men

THE RUBBLE

CHAPTER 1
THE ISOLATED MAN

A man who has friends must himself be friendly, but there is a friend who sticks closer than a brother.

PROVERBS 18:24 (NKJV)

IT was a typical Saturday morning. At the time, it didn't seem like anything out of the ordinary—just a normal conversation with my wife.

"Have you decided about boot camp?"

"It's called Base Camp."

"Okay, have you made a decision about *Base Camp?*" Wendy's gaze bore into me.

"Yeah, and I don't think it's gonna be a good fit."

"Why not?"

"Because I know what's going to happen. Men's retreats are always the same old same old—cigars and small talk for three days. Not interested. Plus, I don't have time right now."

Wendy walked over to our laptop. "Alright, Mr. Negative, sounds like you have it all figured out. But, in case you might be willing to reconsider, maybe I'll just take a peek and see if there are any spots still open."

"Honey, please let it go." I glanced down at my phone.

"Too late." She flashed a smile at me.

"What do you mean, too late? Tell me you didn't do what I think you just did."

Wendy shrugged her shoulders, and held both hands up.

"Great. You realize I can call and cancel the registration."

"Yeah, but you won't." She smiled again.

That smile. That dang smile. She knows it's my kryptonite. How am I ever supposed to win an argument with her when she can flash that thing at any moment? Not fair.

"And I won't cancel my registration and try to get a refund because?"

"Because you and I both know there's a chance that this time might be different, and just the thought of that makes you curious enough to want to go and find out."

Checkmate.

Typical for my wife. Often the voice of reason in my life, and this time was no exception. No exception indeed.

TOXIC COUNSEL

In *The Two Towers*, the second book of *The Lord of the Rings* trilogy, King Theoden seeks counsel from his chief advisor, Grima (1). Theoden is unaware that Grima, otherwise known as Wormtongue, is an agent and spy for the evil wizard, Saruman. With each venomous consultation, Wormtongue's words slowly infect the King's mind. Over time, their poison brings about a gradual decomposition of Theoden's entire being, leaving him on his deathbed.

Theoden desperately needs to be rescued. Thankfully, Gandalf the Great (a good wizard) comes to his aid and breaks the spell. By doing so, Gandalf saves not only the King's life, but the Kingdom of Rohan as well.

For most of my adult life, I received my own toxic counsel. Though it came in numerous forms and from a variety of sources, the message remained the same:

You're on your own—you must rely on yourself for your strength.

Like Theoden, I didn't have a clue about the toll the lies were taking on my heart.

THE LONE RANGER

Through most of my young adult life, I always had a core group of close friends, but once I reached my thirties, things started to change. It became increasingly difficult to maintain contact. Between work and family, it seemed I didn't have time for anything else. Deep down I knew something was missing, but I didn't know what to do about it. So I ignored it and told myself that I really didn't need friends that much. As the years went by, I reached out less and less.

You're on your own—you must rely on yourself for your strength.

From time to time, Wendy challenged me on it. "Do you think you get enough time with friends?"

I usually got defensive and offered the same excuse. "It's just too hard to connect; everyone is so busy."

Eventually she stopped asking, but I failed to notice. I had convinced myself everything was fine. It was all good.

Right.

THE PRIMER

Sometimes in our lives, we encounter a dramatic turning point—a milestone that marks a change in the trajectory of our path. But before that happens, we may need to experience a primer. Primers are scenarios that prepare us for something bigger—something that may ultimately rescue our hearts. Primers can be challenging because they usually involve being vulnerable. One of these primers occurred during a conversation I had with someone one evening at Base Camp.

"So I've got a question for you."
"Go for it."
"Do you ever get lonely?"
I didn't see that one coming. *What kind of question is that?* "Uh, what exactly do you mean when you say 'lonely'?"
"You know, lonely for friendship, lonely for others to share the journey with you?" William said.
For so long, I had convinced myself that I didn't need friendship anymore. Now here I sat, across the table from a virtual stranger, and I was about to tell him something I thought I would never admit to anyone, let alone another guy.

"Um . . . well, when you put it that way. Yeah, I guess you could say that word."

"'That word'?"

Apparently he isn't going to let me off the hook. "Well, okay. Yeah, I am a little lonely sometimes." It felt good to be honest.

"Yeah, me too." He smiled with an expression that spoke of relief.

We had taken off the masks long enough to express what was going on beneath the surface as we sat and talked about our lives for the next hour or so. God was certainly preparing me for what was to come that weekend.

THE BALL AND CHAIN OF ISOLATION

If we're not used to doing it, reaching out can feel pretty awkward. We use our schedules and the demands of our family as reasons to keep from connecting with others. But when we hide behind these excuses, we fail to recognize a common fear that most men have—being vulnerable.

It's just too hard to connect; everyone is so busy.

Wendy and I used to argue about our lack of time together. She would contend that we weren't connecting, and I would argue that we spend plenty of time together. I failed to realize she wasn't really disputing a lack of time, but rather a lack of heart.

I was having an affair with isolation, and it was killing my marriage.

As time passed, we slowly drifted further and further apart. Just coexisting in some sort of parallel universe. I was struggling to come alive and pursue Wendy with passion. Instead, I'd become isolated and resigned to living in survival mode.

Isolation makes us treat our heart like it has some fatal disease that must be quarantined. Nothing gets in, nothing gets out. When we isolate from our brothers and God, we end up isolating from our spouse as well. We may spend time together, but our heart has been walled off. The ball and chain is never really about schedules or the demands of our family. What really stymies us most is isolation itself.

And let us not neglect our meeting together, as some people do, but encourage one another, especially now that the day of his return is drawing near.

HEBREWS 10:25 (NLT)

THE BROTHERING*
INTERACTIVE STUDY QUESTIONS

1. What were your friendships like as a kid? Do you ever remember feeling alone or lonely?

2. How well did your father maintain connection with others?

3. What qualities make a good friend?

4. How often do you spend time with others presently?

5. How do you spend the time together? What, if anything, is missing?

6. How does isolation impact your marriage or significant other?

7. How does isolation impact your relationship with God?

* *The Brothering Interactive Study Questions* are just that—interactive. It is preferable that they be done in a group setting with other men.

THE FATHERING*

My son,
You have become isolated from others.
Isolated from me.
This is how you have chosen to protect your heart.
But isolating yourself has not kept your heart from
hurt and pain.
Walling yourself up only brings you more pain.
In your efforts to protect yourself, you end up
starving yourself.
Starving yourself of my love.
It's time for you to let your heart be known again, son.
Let my fathering into your heart through my Spirit.
Let my fathering into your heart through those I place
along your path.
The evil one wants you to believe that others are
not trustworthy.
That I am not trustworthy.
But you know I AM.
Trust me and know that I am with you.

I love you, son.
Dad

*The Fathering—Words from the Father meditations are based on the scriptures presented in their corresponding chapters. These are meant to draw us into the Father's love for us as His sons. Take time to let God Father you as you read them and allow others to read them to you.

A SON'S PRAYER*

Father,
Please give me courage as I pray this prayer.
I confess I have isolated myself from others.
I confess I have even isolated myself from you.
Please forgive me.
I confess I have allowed fear to be my guide at times.
Fear of _____ (rejection, abandonment,
being looked upon as weak, etc.).
Oh, Father, I am weak.
Help me to allow you and others into my weakness.
Help me to stop pretending I'm strong all the time.
Let me experience your strength.
Let me experience your forgiveness.
Father, please give me courage to take down this wall
around my heart.
Thank you for your unwavering love and patience.

I love you, Dad.
Amen

---

*A Son's Prayer are prayers meant to lead us into a more intimate and vulnerable interaction with Father God. Though not meant as any kind of formula, these prayers are designed to foster more transparency with God about the rubble in our lives as well as our desperate need for His Fathering.

THE RUBBLE

CHAPTER 2
THE FATHERLESS MAN

A father of the fatherless, a defender of widows, is God in His holy habitation.

PSALM 68:5 (NKJV)

I could hear him take another swig. I hated that sound. I knew what it led to. Still in its paper bag, the bottle of scotch made a thud as he put it back on the shelf under the bar. Another Sunday night and another episode of *Hee Haw* as my father made his usual transformation into an asshole. Alcohol has a way of doing that to people who drink too much.

This particular night he'd had a little more than usual.

"Look at the pair on that one," Dad said. Only he didn't use the word "pair". *Hee Haw*, a 1970s country music variety show was not, shall we say, all about the music. Being a sensitive kid, something inside me knew it was wrong to degrade women like that. I was a young boy trying to make sense of the female body, and now my alcoholic father was giving me a lesson in human anatomy.

I hated him for it. I hated him for a lot of things. I hated him for keeping pornography in the house and burdening me with the temptation that came with it. I hated him for smoking, drinking, and using vulgar language. But most of all, I hated him for what he did to my mother. Many times she'd cry up in their bedroom, while my father stayed out drinking until early in the morning. To drown out her sobbing, I stayed down in the basement watching countless hours of television with the volume turned way up. Eventually, I felt it was my duty to go upstairs and comfort her. Someone had to. I hated being put into that role. After all, I was just a kid.

Years later, after my mother had died, I got a call from a woman who was dating my father. "Your dad's in detox. You'd better come and pick him up." Apparently she'd had enough. So had I. After years of pent-up anger, I unloaded on him that evening.

"When are you going to stop doing this? When are you going to get your shit together? I'm tired of taking care of you—I'm not doing this anymore. You're going to have to get someone else to clean up after you, Dad. I'm done!"

That someone else turned out to be my sister.

Later that summer my father suffered a stroke. The doctors said it was probably due to all the drinking he'd done through the years. I talked it over with my sister, and we decided to move him out to where she lived on the West Coast. We hoped a new setting would give him a fresh start. It didn't. His alcoholism only escalated. It got to the point where she and my brother-in-law didn't know where he was or even if he was alive. My sister went through hell during this time with my father. I hated him for putting her through that. At times, I wished he were dead.

Be careful what you wish for. My father died later that year.

The feeling that came with this loss was like an ache—deep and raw. But the real problem wasn't the emotional pain; it was the pain's anchor point—hatred. My father was dead, but my hatred was alive and well. And it was eating away at my heart and soul.

THE RUBBLE OF HATRED

Hatred is like a boomerang. It tends to come back around and hit us upside the head. This is why God commands us not to do it. It serves no purpose.

> *You shall not hate your brother in your heart. You shall surely rebuke your neighbor, and not bear sin because of him. You shall not take vengeance, nor bear any grudge against the children of your people, but you shall love your neighbor as yourself: I am the Lord.*
>
> LEVITICUS 19:17-18 (NKJV)

When we choose to hate someone, we end up creating a monster. Remember Dr. Frankenstein? Inevitably, the monster turns on us, and we end up hating ourselves, as well. Hatred doesn't differentiate between victim and perpetrator— all are its victims. As I contemplated this, God gave me a picture of two brothers traveling with their father along the backwards journey.

THE BACKWARDS JOURNEY

Saddled up and riding alongside each other, Cody and his brother headed down the trail with nothing but blue skies overhead.

Cody noticed first. "Where's Dad?" He asked.

"I don't know. He was just in front of us a minute ago." Roy glanced around.

"Dad, where are you?" They both yelled simultaneously, by accident, which made them laugh.

Then they heard their father's voice. "I'm right behind you, boys."

As they turned toward their father, relief gave way to uneasiness as they saw dark clouds forming in the distance.

"Looks like there's gonna be a heck of a storm, Dad. Are you sure you want to go that way?" Cody asked.

"Yep." He said calmly.

"Why would we ever want to head that way when we have blue skies in front of us?" Roy had a panicked look on his face.

"I guess you're gonna have to trust me on this one, guys."

Cody sat on his horse for a minute staring at the ominous clouds on the horizon. He debated whether to follow his father into the storm or whether to turn and ride the other way into clear skies.

"C'mon, Cody." Roy said, trying to be strong for his brother. Unsure of where they were headed, their fears were replaced by a newfound strength as they rode alongside their father, shoulder to shoulder, into the eye of the storm. There was no place they would rather be.

As I contemplated this picture, it became clear that I, too, was trying to steer clear of the dark clouds of my past. I thought I could avoid it by just focusing on the road ahead. Like Cody and Roy's father, my heavenly Father knew I needed to go on a backwards journey in order to put the past in its proper place. Many of us need to confront parts of our past in order for us to gain enough traction to move forward. It may be difficult to resist the temptation to be passive about this.

Just give it some time. After all, time heals all wounds.

Whoever said that was probably in some serious denial. Time doesn't heal all wounds, but God does.

A number of years ago, I was fortunate to be a part of a men's group where I first started to experience what I now understand as brothering and fathering. Through newly-formed relationships with these brothers, God taught me and brought healing that fathered me in the process of forgiving my father. On one occasion, one of the men talked about how repentance plays a powerful role in the process of forgiving someone who has hurt us. No matter how much we've been hurt, we are responsible for our response to the hurt. Ironically, if I wanted to be rescued from my hatred, that liberation would not be found through forgiveness alone, but through repenting of the sin of hating my father.

So I decided to make a trip to Montevideo, Minnesota.

THE ROAD LESS TRAVELED

It was a beautiful spring morning. As I drove to the gravesite, I really didn't know what to expect. The expansive cemetery had gravestones in every direction in what seemed like endless rows. The whole time I was there I saw no one else except someone cutting the grass. It had been five years since my sister and I had buried my father, and this trip marked my first return to his grave. As I drove up to the row where my parents' gravestones were located, memories of the burial service flooded my mind.

"Is there anything anyone would like to say about Paul? Perhaps a fond memory or a story about his life?" My brother-in-law scanned the small gathering of family.

Silence.

Not a single word. I couldn't think of one word to say. I certainly didn't feel sad. Rather, hatred was right there advising me like a snake slithering around my neck.

"You were the victim. You don't owe him anything. He doesn't deserve it." It hissed.

My trance quickly broke when the groundskeeper started a lawnmower in the distance. The memory of the funeral faded as I reoriented myself. Then I noticed something. A lump in my throat. The lump gave way to tears, as I stared at the gravestones. Then I spoke to the one I had come to ask forgiveness from.

"I have hated you for a long time, Dad."

Silence.

"I hated you for what you did to me. For what you did to mom. I wanted you to feel the hurt that I felt so I shut you out of my life. But I never took the time to put myself in your shoes and consider the demons you wrestled with. Oh, how you must have fought it. How it must have tormented you. I had no clue. All I could see was the hatred. I couldn't see you, Dad. I couldn't see you. Please forgive me." Then it was silent as I wept.

It was in that silence that a picture emerged. My parents stood there now, just a few feet away. Tears streaming down their faces as they looked at me with sadness in their eyes. I could tell they understood what I had suffered through all those years as a young boy. Then their sadness turned to fondness as they smiled at me tenderly. I wanted the moment to last forever.

Then the picture faded and they were gone.

As I got into my car, I took one last look at the grave markers in my rearview mirror as I drove out of the cemetery. As I thanked God for what just happened, He posed a question.

"Where is your hatred for your father?"

I quickly scanned my past, pouring through memory after memory. I looked for any sign of hatred or even anger.

I searched and searched trying to find it. But I could not. The hatred was gone.

THE FATHERLESS JOURNEY

Journeying into certain parts of our past can be uncomfortable and sometimes extremely painful. Words like journey, path, trail, road, etc., all suggest the same trajectory—forward. It doesn't seem logical to go backward in order to go forward. But when we've lost something along the way, we have no other alternative. At one point or another, all of us contend with fatherlessness—a lack of connection with God as Father. Fatherlessness had occurred in my life not because I had lost my dad, but because I had allowed things like hatred to get in the way of God fathering me.

The fatherless man cannot save or find himself. He is a leaf in the wind, blown this way and that. But a fathered man is rescued from the rubble and begins a new journey along a road of redemption in his life. We desperately need God to father us. Rescue and redemption cannot occur without it. And God's fathering, in many cases, happens in the context of relationship through the brothering of men. In fact, it is this paradigm that sets us free to experience the fathering of God in a radical, new way.

They wandered in the wilderness in a desolate way; they found no city to dwell in. Hungry and thirsty, their soul fainted in them.

Then they cried out to the LORD in their trouble, and He delivered them out of their distresses. And He led them forth by the right way, that they might go to a city for a dwelling place.

PSALM 107:4-7 (NKJV)

THE BROTHERING
INTERACTIVE STUDY QUESTIONS

1. Describe your relationship with your father during childhood. How did your father meet your physical, emotional and spiritual needs?

2. How did your father validate you as a young man?

3. Describe times when your father hurt you or other significant men in your life have wounded you, including times when your father was passive and unavailable either emotionally or physically.

4. Describe your relationship with God the Father?

5. In what ways has your journey been fatherless? In other words, what has gotten in the way of God's fathering in your life—both past and present?

6. What specific areas of your life need more of God's fathering right now?

THE FATHERING

My son,

I have watched you try to do life on your own and in your own strength.

Son, let me father you and give you what you need.

I will take you out of your suffering.

Trust me, son.

I know that over the years your heart has been hurt.

I have heard the bitter words in your heart towards those who have hurt you.

Bitterness, judgment, and resentment have robbed you of my fathering.

Remember, I cannot forgive your sin if you are not willing to forgive another.

Bring these hurts and injustices to me.

Let me come into your struggle, whatever it may be, and father you.

Allow me to lead you on your journey.

Let's ride together on the greatest adventure ever known.

I love you with all my heart, son.

Dad

A SON'S PRAYER

Father,

I'm unsure how to pray.

Please show me how.

I want to trust you, but I'm so used to relying on myself.

I have essentially lived a fatherless life; not allowing you to father me in all that I do.

Please forgive me.

Please reveal what I have harbored in my heart towards you, others and myself that would rob me of your presence (bitterness, judgments, resentment, hatred, etc.).

Please grant me the courage to confess these things and ask for forgiveness as I become more aware of them.

I realize this is a process.

Thank you for calling me your son.

I accept the work Jesus did on the cross for me so I can come to you and call you "Father".

So that I can call you "Dad".

I want to gain a deeper understanding of what it means to be your son and for you to be my Father.

I want to ride with you on this great adventure.

I love you, Dad.

Amen

THE RUBBLE

CHAPTER 3
THE SHAME-FILLED MAN

They looked to Him and were radiant, and their faces were not ashamed.

PSALM 34:5 (NKJV)

IF a man wants to shed his Lone Ranger persona and find a band of brothers, sooner or later he must allow himself to become vulnerable. This presents a dilemma. He doesn't want to go the journey alone, but he doesn't want to look needy either.

And therein lies one of man's greatest fears—looking weak.

There are few things we hate more. Because associated with appearing weak is something horribly debilitating and toxic—shame. Shame goes beyond implicating behavior. Shame gets personal. It doesn't just imply we did something bad, it says we *are* bad. Shame poses the threat of rejection bringing with it an indictment of our entire being.

If people knew the real you, they would reject you.

The research doesn't paint a real picture of health when it comes to men and their emotions.

Men have more difficulty expressing emotions than women do. Men also attempt to exert greater control over the expression of emotions. With the exception of anger, men often look at being emotional as a sign of weakness.

- Men spend more time ruminating over negative emotions.

- Men share their emotions with far less frequency than women.
- Men use less emotional language and fewer "emotion" words.
- Men are more likely to under-report negative feelings.
- Men are more willing to express pride, anger and jealousy (2).

For most men, expressing emotion has become inextricably linked with shame. So we cover our emotions with pretense and numb them with our addictions until we no longer feel anything. With mockery and condemnation, shame buries us in silence while scolding us for even entertaining the notion of rescue.

THE TOXICITY OF SHAME

It's common for feelings of shame to originate in childhood. As children, we're meant to experience vulnerability in safe, non-judgmental environments. If a child receives ridicule and rejection in place of unconditional love, vulnerability then becomes associated with a strong sense of shame. The child learns quickly that the only way to avoid shame is to avoid being vulnerable. When this occurs during childhood, it sets a precedent for the rest of our lives. Let's take a look at a couple examples.

Johnny starts to cry after he falls off his bike, but instead of receiving comfort from his father, his dad says something that crushes his spirit. (Notice his father's words attack Johnny himself, not his behavior.) "Don't be such a baby! Stop crying! You're not going to die!"

Terrified of going to school for fear of being bullied once again by a kid twice his size, Travis finds little support and understanding from his father. Instead, he encounters his dad's disdain for weakness. "C'mon, Travis. Don't be such a wimp. Stand up to him like a man!"

Whatever the story, shame draws the same conclusion for us.

Don't let them see you sweat. Don't let them see you weak. Don't let them see you (the real you) period.

But it goes even deeper than ridicule or rejection.

SO I BECAME HARD...

I come from a violent background. So I became hard. I realized that I had made myself that way to deal with a feeling of abandonment and shame (3).

—MICKEY ROURKE

If the insinuation of shame is you are bad, the implication is you are not wanted and you are alone. What a devastating one-two punch. Look at any example of bullying. Someone is being picked on because they are perceived as weak. It starts with intimidation and ridicule, but it usually ends with some form of alienation and abandonment. Pop culture teaches us that no one wants to be associated with someone who is looked upon as the victim or loser. We are taught at a young age to side with the victor. The conqueror! The most powerful! This is what gives the bully power—the fear of ridicule and the threat of abandonment.

Dysfunctional families operate much the same way. Parents who have difficulty expressing their own feelings will often respond with ridicule and disconnect when the child expresses his. We tend to distance ourselves from that which is foreign to us. The child often interprets the distancing, usually done through silence, as abandonment. The child learns that showing weakness means he will be rejected. Here it is again. Boy, this thing just gets hammered into us! We can't escape it. If not at home, we encounter it at school or somewhere else. Any young boy is left to conclude that he can never be weak for fear of rejection and abandonment. Yet, he knows on some level that he is weak. So what does he do?

He hides his true self from others.

To cope with fears of rejection and abandonment, we keep our hopes, dreams, fantasies, fears, doubts, loves, passions, sadness, discouragement and pretty much any struggle we may have hidden behind walls erected by shame. We may maintain some relationships, but we make sure we keep them shallow and superficial.

This way no one gets hurt. But we are mistaken.

THE HUNGRY HEART CONUNDRUM

The toxicity of shame and the toll it takes on our heart is more than we can imagine. Shame burrows in and tells a man to keep his heart hidden from others for fear of rejection. But if he chooses to hide his heart from others, he will not be known. This creates a nasty catch-22. Like all men, we were created with the fundamental need to be known.

There is no end to the diverse arts men practise to get some food for their soul; and to whatever course they turn themselves, you will see, as clearly as possible, that they are hungry (4).

—UNKNOWN

We work so hard at making sure we're protecting our heart from rejection, yet by doing so we end up starving our soul. In other words, we reject ourselves in order to protect ourselves from the rejection of others. How tragically ironic.

If the man of shame wants to find rescue and redemption, he must confront the lies that shame has told him about himself. This is not something easily remedied by positive self-talk. We cannot talk ourselves out of shame. We must experience the truth of who we truly are in the context of relationship so the lies of shame can be powerfully countered and conquered through an alternate experience. Shame gets its power by keeping our hearts hidden from others. Conversely, shame loses its power through our being unconditionally loved by others. When we allow God to father us experientially through our brothers with His unconditional love, we overcome shame and begin to understand who we truly are as men. Our souls no longer starve. Instead, they are now quenched, as we experience the fathering of God through the brothering of men.

THE BROTHERING
INTERACTIVE STUDY QUESTIONS

1. Describe an occasion in your childhood when you remember feeling ridiculed or rejected.

2. How did that experience shape your views on being vulnerable with others?

3. How much does your performance (work, athletics, etc.) play a role in determining your worth and value as a man?

4. If someone showed you unconditional love, what might it look like?

5. What areas in your life have been the most affected by shame? How has shame made its impact?

6. Talk about a specific struggle that has caused a considerable amount of shame in your life.

THE FATHERING

My son,

Come to me now and let me give you courage, son.

Let me give you strength to take down the walls you've built around your heart.

Let's demolish them together—you and me—one brick at a time.

The evil one has lied to you and used shame to harden your heart.

You've been told that you are not good enough.

You've been called names and even called yourself names that have harmed you.

My Son died for you on the cross so that you wouldn't be defined by your sin.

Come to me as you are; bring me your shame and all its messages.

Let my fathering come into your heart now and begin to heal you from your shame.

Let me give you a new name.

Let your heart receive my words when I call you "son."

You are my son.

My son, whom I love dearly.

I love you.

Dad

A SON'S PRAYER

Father,

Please help me find your courage now as I pray.

Help me take down these walls I've built around my heart.

I have been so fearful of rejection and what others would
think of me if I showed weakness.

Sadly, I have rejected myself more than anyone else has.

I've been so afraid of showing others that I'm weak.

Truth is, I am weak.

Dad, please be my strength.

I invite you into the mess of my shame.

I can't fix it. I can't rid myself of it no matter how hard I try.

Help me receive your unconditional love so that shame will
no longer have power in my life.

Help me receive your unconditional love through the brothers
you put in my life.

Help me receive the identity you have for me as your son.

And let that define me instead of my performance
or accomplishments.

Thank you, Jesus, for dying on the cross so I wouldn't be
identified by my sin any longer.

Thank you for loving me.

Thank you for making me your son and for being my Dad.

I love you.

Amen

THE RUBBLE

CHAPTER 4
THE ADDICTED MAN

Therefore let him who thinks he stands take heed lest he fall. No temptation has overtaken you except such as is common to man; but God is faithful, who will not allow you to be tempted beyond what you are able, but with the temptation will also make the way of escape, that you may be able to bear it.

1 CORINTHIANS 10:12-13 (NKJV)

RALPH'S STORY

What the hell am I doing here? How did I get to where I am?

It's been three days. I'm alone and there's a chill in the air even though it's mid July. I'm lying on a picnic table looking at all the stars in the night sky—stars I've never seen before—and I'm crying out to God.

There has got to be more to life than this.

Yes, it's been three days since I had a drink and five more to go until I'll be home. I'm on a church mission trip—a challenge from my pastor. "Just go on one mission trip. It will change your life." He said. I'm in Cody, Wyoming, a part of the country I've come to love—the Wild West, the Rockies, endless mountain views, dirt roads and trails leading to what seems to nowhere, a place to explore and find adventure.

But first, I need to take you back a bit, to an October morning in 1994 when I saw the snowcapped peaks of the Rockies for the first time, a time when God spoke to me in a way that got my attention. We had been up 20 or so hours, driving all night, trailer in tow and our hunting gear in the back of the Toyota 4-Runner. My first elk hunt, with two of my old drinking buddies. With a fifth of Jim Beam in one hand and a Diet Coke in the other, I watched the sun come up from the east as we pulled off of I-70 west of Denver. It appeared as though God's light was shining down as the sun's rays hit the snowcapped peaks of the Rockies.

"I have something for you to do in Colorado." God said.

What? God doesn't speak to drunks, does He?

That encounter has haunted me ever since that cold October morning. But this story started even earlier than that. Much earlier.

I remember the morning my dad instructed me to scrape down the house. The paint had started to peel, and I needed to get it ready for the painter who was coming in a few days. Like any other 9 or 10-year-old boy, I had a few questions.

"Where's the ladder? What about a scraper or wire brush? How do I do this, Dad?"
"Figure it out, son." His only words.

Such was my dad's way of making me think on my own and teaching me not to depend on others for help—to learn how to do things for myself. So I worked on the house all day, so proud of the job I'd done—all on my own. Then Dad got home, probably with a few drinks already under his belt. He got out of his car, looked up at the house and said something that has stayed with me all these years.

"You missed some spots."

He didn't say another word before he walked into the house. All I could think was that I didn't work hard enough or smart enough, or I didn't pay close enough attention to what I was doing. In my mind I was a failure.

That's just one of many stories from childhood where I was left to figure things out on my own. Being forced to do so made me strong and very independent. But it has also caused me to think too much—something I still struggle with today. My mind would never stop. Then, at age 15, I found alcohol, and, for the next 30 years, drinking offered rest and escape from the pressures I allowed others to put on me, as well as the pressures I put on myself. I figured if drinking worked for Dad, it would work for me.

My father was a good man, a very good provider. He taught me things he thought would help me make it in life—things like having a strong work ethic, being honest, looking a man in the eye when you talk to him, having a firm hand shake, always having a way out, walking with integrity, being comfortable no matter what setting you're in, having a caring heart to show compassion toward others.

I can still hear his words today: "Just do the right thing, son, and everything else will take care of itself."

My father was also an alcoholic. I can't recall seeing him drunk or him missing a day of work due to a hangover, but he depended on alcohol to get him through the day. And he passed this habit on to his son. And just like my dad, over the years drinking became a daily habit for me, as well.

And then one day, Dad quit drinking, just like that.

Afterward, from time to time, he would ask me, "You still drinking son?"

"Yes, sir, Daddy, I am." I would say while looking him right in the eye.

"If you keep it up, son, that damn stuff is gonna kill you someday."

If you remember, this story started with me in Cody, Wyoming, lying on that picnic table. That was in 2003. By that point, I'd had multiple drinks every day for nearly 30 years. Through those years I traveled to Colorado at least once and sometimes two or three times a year. It became a special place for me to spend time with God. But after that mission trip, something was different. On that trip I had a clear mind, a better understanding of what God was up to.

Shortly after that mission trip, I ran into my pastor one afternoon. As I placed my daily 12-pack of beer on the counter in the little country store, he walked in. We exchanged small talk, and then went our separate ways. When I arrived back home, I looked at that 12-pack sitting on my seat. I didn't drink a single beer that night. And from that day on, every time I bought a beer, I saw my pastor's face.

And then one day, I just quit drinking.

But my journey had started a few days before that beautiful spring day in the Rockies of Colorado. It began while I was at home in Mississippi, full of excitement, as I got ready for a spring break ski trip with two of my old drinking buddies. God calmly tapped me on the shoulder.

"Oh, by the way, when you leave Colorado this time, you're not going to drink anymore."

His casual demeanor caught me by surprise. "Say what?"

We had a great week of skiing, fellowship and drinking. As we pulled out of Monarch, Colorado, to head home, a sense of sadness came over me. I knew my life would soon change. What did God have in store for me? We both knew that my addiction to alcohol had kept me from being able to do things He had planned for me to do even before I was born. As I drove south on I-25 in Colorado and approached Raton Pass, I could see the sign "Welcome to New Mexico." Emotions overcame this ol' broken soul of a man.

What did my Father have planned for me?

As we went under the bridge out of Colorado and into New Mexico, I had my last drink. That was March 15, 2004.

RALPH K. MCLELLAND

Confess your sins one to another and pray for each other so that you may be healed.

JAMES 5:16A (NLT)

NO ONE IS IMMUNE

What a powerful testimony of God's fathering. When Ralph shared this part of his story with me, I thought of how most of us struggle with at least one addiction or another at some point in our lives. But why? Because they work—at least, initially. They help us escape pain, boredom, anxiety, shame, etc. And just as general anesthesia doesn't discriminate its effect on different parts of the body, nor does our soul-numbing lifestyle choose which emotion to numb. All are numbed.

I never realized how addicted I was to my cell phone until a couple of years ago when I dropped it and cracked the screen. It just slipped off the counter, and I heard the sickening sound of shattered glass. My first instinct was to call my wife, but she was out of the country at the time. Then it hit me. I don't have one phone number memorized besides Wendy's. I could use email to communicate, but that felt as expedient as sending up a smoke signal. I felt helpless and alone. It disturbed me to realize how dependent I had become on this little device.

Why do I need this thing so much?

Obviously, I depended on it for the purpose of connecting with others. But my phone provided something else that I wasn't even aware of until it became inoperable.

THE NEW HEROIN

When discussing addiction, we often refer to the usual suspects: alcohol, illicit drugs, tobacco, gambling, pornography, etc. Yet there's another that's rarely discussed—one that impacts us all.

Busyness.

We have to work more than we ever have before. Our children get involved in activities that require participation seven days a week, morning, noon and night. We make sure our schedules are always filled, or we feel unproductive. What we don't seem to have a lot of time for is silence. Some refer to it as having quiet time. But how quiet is it, really? I must confess my quiet time is often spent making one request after another. When does Father God have a moment to get a word in edgewise? Being quiet is more than just a struggle sometimes. It can be a battle. Though I call myself a human being, sadly, I live my life more as a human doing. I find it uncomfortable just being with God in the silence. And I don't think I'm alone here.

I often hear people say they intentionally keep busy so they don't have to hear themselves think. This gives at least one explanation why we don't like being in listener mode with God—we don't know what to do with our thoughts. Then one day the light bulb went on—invite God into the thoughts.

Then Jesus said, "Come to me, all of you who are weary and carry heavy burdens, and I will give you rest. Take my yoke upon you. Let me teach you, because I am humble and gentle at heart, and you will find rest for your souls. For my yoke is easy to bear, and the burden I give you is light."

MATTHEW 11:28-30 (NLT)

God knows about our struggle to focus amidst all the busyness. What I didn't understand was His simple desire just to be with me—thoughts and all. I found that when I invited Him into the thoughts, my prayer time was more peaceful and focused. And more intimate, which only made sense. How can we connect when we're distracted? We can't. And there it is— the antidote for virtually any addiction.

Intimacy.

SEX VS. INTIMACY

God created man to have intimate relationships—relationships that allow us to share deeply from the heart, without fear of being judged.

As I have listened to hundreds, if not thousands of men's stories through the years as a psychologist, one thing is often missing in a man's life—deep friendships. When intimate connections—with others and God—don't happen on a regular basis, a man's unmet emotional needs often become sexualized. It then should come as no surprise that most of us have struggled with pornography at one time or another. Sexual addiction is rampant in our culture, in part due to its easy access via the Internet. All the behavior modification programming in the world won't make any difference if we don't live intimate lives. One resource tells us we need to recite certain scriptures. Another urges us to "bounce" our eyes away from the source of temptation. You can bounce all you want, but you still need intimacy.

It's interesting that the words intimacy and sex are often used interchangeably. But they are not the same. Intimacy is about connection. Period. It has nothing to do with the physical act of sex. If sex comes from a spiritually and emotionally connected place where there is love and respect, then by all means call it intimacy. But if it's just about having intercourse, then don't call it intimacy. It's just sex.

When patients discuss their struggle with pornography, I usually ask them this question. "How much do you share with others (including your spouse) about what you think, feel and need?" Almost without exception the response is the same. "I don't share personal aspects of my life with anyone. No one really knows me."

Being addicted to a life of isolation precludes us from having any intimacy with anyone—including God. This provides a major set-up for addictive behavior. As we isolate ourselves from others, our loneliness increases. As loneliness increases, our urge to numb the loneliness with addictive behavior increases. With the increase in addictive behavior comes a sense of shame and secrecy, which leads to more isolation. Then the pattern repeats itself again and again.

It wasn't until I started allowing God's fathering into my life through my brothers that I started to deal with my loneliness. As I addressed the loneliness in my life, shame and isolation became less and less prevalent. My marriage became more passionate and intimate. Coupled with emotional and spiritual intimacy, sex became a vehicle of expression for the love I had for my wife.

We must break the pattern or the cycle will continue to bury us in the rubble. The key is and always will be—intimacy.

INTIMACY WITH GOD

At the end of this chapter, like the other chapters in this book, I include a sample prayer that can be used as a catalyst for deeper intimacy with God. Some of it involves speaking and some of it listening. This is not a formula—just something that works for me. In addition, I would encourage you to invite God into your struggle no matter what it might be. Sometimes it helps to ask Him for a visual image before inviting Him into it. Begin by asking God for a picture that represents your struggle at its worst. Then invite Him into that picture and notice what happens. Ask Father God to speak to you as his son. Again, notice what happens.

Developing intimacy with God is a process of confessing, watching and listening. It takes willingness and vulnerability. The listening part might feel strange and a bit awkward. If you feel this way, you're not alone. It might also seem a bit awkward to invite God into thoughts that contain unwanted sexual content, for example. Actually, it makes all the sense in the world. Our destructive thoughts are part of our rubble. How can we be rescued if the first responders are not allowed to enter the rubble? Not possible. We most certainly cannot dig ourselves out. God knows our thoughts anyway.

O LORD, you have examined my heart and know everything about me. You know when I sit down or stand up. You know my thoughts even when I'm far away. You see me when I travel and

when I rest at home. You know everything I do. You know what
I am going to say even before I say it, LORD.

PSALM 139:1-4 (NLT)

Often, we believe we've won the battle if we simply eliminate the behavior. However, this myopic assessment of the problem never provides a long-term solution. The symptoms may be dormant, but the problem still exists if we continue lacking intimate relationships in our lives.

THE BROTHERING
INTERACTIVE STUDY QUESTIONS

1. How does busyness interfere with your relationships (intimacy) with others?

2. What part of Ralph's story resonated with you? Why?

3. In what ways have you tried to rescue yourself from your own addictive behavior?

4. How much do you share about your addictive behavior with others?

5. How does your tendency to isolate from others play a role in your addictive behavior?

6. Take time to share some of your struggle with addictive behavior. What is it like to talk about this with others?

7. Take some time to listen to God right now. Invite Him into your unwanted thoughts for the next five minutes or so. What is it like for you to just be quiet and listen to Father God?

THE FATHERING

My son,

Come to me.

I'm sad about your struggle with addiction.

I know this has caused you such pain and strife.

Although I am sad about what this has done to your heart,
I'm not ashamed of you.

When you separate yourself from me because of shame, it
does you no good.

I cannot help you if you choose isolation over intimacy with
me and with others.

Let me into your struggle, son.

Let me into your rubble.

Let me rescue you.

I will free you as you allow yourself to become vulnerable
with me.

Let me father you, son.

I love you.

Dad

A SON'S PRAYER

Father,
It's difficult for me to stay focused.
My life is so controlled by busyness.
I need you to rescue me.
Here's what I'm thinking right now. (Say your thoughts
out loud, if necessary.)
Please come into these thoughts and bring me your
peace, Father.
Here are my addictive behaviors/thoughts. (Say them out
loud, if necessary.)
These are hard for me to confess. Shame wants to silence me.
Please give me courage, Father.
Please come into these thoughts.
I know that I can't rescue myself from the rubble, Dad.
Please help me see you coming into my struggles as I confess
them. (Take time now to allow God to father you in this
moment.)
Give me courage to live an intimate life that is more
connected with you and others.
Thank you for loving me.

I love you, Dad.
Amen

THE RUBBLE

CHAPTER 5
THE PASSIVE MAN

But let your 'Yes' be 'Yes,' and your 'No,' 'No.' For whatever is more than these is from the evil one.

MATTHEW 5:37 (NKJV)

My father struggled to find his way. Caught up in the rat race trying to provide for his family, he operated in survival mode much of the time. Had he experienced the fathering of God through the brothering of men, he could have discovered his true self. He would have known who he was because he would have understood *whose* he was. Sadly, my father failed to understand that God was trying to get a message to him.

You are my son. You can do all things because I will be your strength. I will never leave you.

This message could have changed his life and altered the trajectory of his path. This message could have impacted how he lived and how he loved those around him. This message could have altered my path because it altered his. Consciously or not, all fathers invite their sons into their journey, and we follow because we simply can't resist. Our DNA dictates our path. Unless God's fathering intervenes and helps us navigate a new path, we will most likely take the road our fathers traveled— even at our own peril. Despite our most heroic human effort, we typically default to what we know, so we imitate our fathers. I can remember making a promise to myself at an early age.

I will never be like him.

Through the years I occasionally took inventory and compared my life to his:

✓ successful career
✓ born-again Christian
✓ reasonably physically fit
✓ not an alcoholic

Though I tried with all my might to be different from my father, I couldn't escape the fact that I was becoming just like him. I turned out to be just as lonely, just as isolated and just as caught up in survival mode. On the outside, I maintained an image of strength and confidence, but the inside revealed a different story. Like my father, I was a passive man.

THE PERIL OF PASSIVITY

I can remember the day I met my wife for the first time. She walked up to me with those captivating blue eyes, and that's all it took. Truly, love at first sight. The infatuation phase carried us nicely for a while. But in retrospect, beneath it all, we both struggled to know who we were. As the years went by, our relationship fell victim to one of the most common diseases of the soul—resignation or passivity. As it is with so many marriages, we stopped pursuing each other with passion. We maintained a friendship, but we gave up on having an intimate, vulnerable relationship.

A few years ago, I wrote a love song for her about a man who struggled to verbalize his feelings for the woman he loved. It wasn't until I started writing this book that I reflected on the song and its true meaning dawned on me. This song really exposed my passivity. Akin to someone stranded on a deserted island, the passionate man inside of me was desperately trying to send a message in a bottle to Wendy. But the bottle got lost at sea for a number of years.

LOOK INTO MY EYES

© 2013 THOMAS MILLS

How can I put all this love into words?
How can I make you see?
How can I explain what I really mean?
I try and write you a love song
But the words come out all wrong
Empty without any meaning
So I'll show you in my own way
And set these feelings free
(Chorus)
So look into my eyes
Baby you will know
Just how much I love you
More than words could ever show
Look into my eyes
See what my heart is saying
Nothing can conceal how I really feel
When you look into my eyes

(Verse 2)
I get so tongue-tied when I see those blue eyes
All I can do is smile
And kiss your lips and hold you for a while
If these arms could tell you
Every time they have held you
All the things that you are to me
They'd have to hold you forever
To mention everything

We had grown further and further apart. Our marriage had continued, but our intimacy had dramatically subsided. We were physically present, but emotionally and spiritually distant.

Just avoid conflict, and keep her happy.

My efforts to avoid conflict at all costs practically cost me my marriage.

When I was a child, I spoke as a child, I understood as a child, I thought as a child; but when I became a man, I put away childish things.

1 CORINTHIANS 13:11 (NKJV)

HAPPY WIFE, HAPPY LIFE

Women don't want men to appease them any more than they want to be married to a golden retriever. My wife wanted a man who knew who he was. One who wasn't afraid to express his feelings and needs, even if hearing them made her angry. She wanted to know that her anger wouldn't make me run away and that I would pursue her even when she wasn't being sweet and nice. After all, what kind of relationship do we have if it's predicated on placating and pacifying one another?

Answer: A false one.

My wife had her own way of protecting herself when we argued. We affectionately named it the "dragon". When the dragon came out, Wendy criticized me. The more critical she was, the more passive and avoidant I became. The more passive I was, the more it triggered the dragon. And so it went. Neither the dragon nor my passivity offered any real defense. We hurt each other more than we protected ourselves. Deep inside, Wendy wanted the man in me to rise up and rescue her from the dragon. Only problem was, I had no fight left in me.

The man in me was dying to love his wife with passion, but my passivity was running the show. And this dynamic wasn't going to change simply by reading a book on love languages or communication skills. No matter how insightful the material might be, no amount of information by itself could rescue my marriage.

When we operate out of passivity, it forces our spouse into a parental role. The spouse loses respect for her husband because he is no longer the man she married, but a child she must take care of. The opposite is also true. When a man begins to discover who he is, he operates out of love and not passivity. His spouse becomes drawn to his passion, and the pressure to assume a parental role dissipates. As God's fathering rescues and redeems us, we are then able to offer our fathered (masculine) identity to our brides. Our wife is no longer the source of our identity and approval. Our identity only comes from the Father. My wife's pursuit of my masculine strength exposed the shadow man that existed in me—one who operated out of isolation and self-reliance.

You're on your own—you must rely on yourself for your strength.

We must allow God's fathering into our life, or the passive man will rule us. Fear of other's disapproval becomes less and less our master because we have our Father's approval.

There is no room in love for fear. Well-formed love banishes fear. Since fear is crippling, a fearful life—fear of death, fear of judgment—is one not yet fully formed in love.

1 JOHN 4:18 (MSG)

THE SHADOW MAN

To fully break the chains of passivity we must contend with a little lie that packs a big punch to our masculinity.

Just be nice and nobody will get hurt.

Here in the Land of 10,000 Lakes, where I live, we have an expression to describe our hospitality—Minnesota Nice. Though this approach might work well at the local visitor center, it doesn't get us very far in relationships. When we are passive, we fixate on pleasing others. If we must always please, we cannot be honest. If we cannot be honest, we cannot be known. If we cannot be known, we have no intimacy. If we have no connection with others, we become susceptible to more rubble in our lives. Without having real intimacy we resort to addictive behavior to try and fill the void.

Passivity cuts us at the knees and takes us out of the race. We stop living from the heart. We stop saying what we really think for fear of provoking any type of conflict—especially with our spouse. We think as long as she doesn't get pissed off, we're good. As long as she gives us the thumbs up, we're winning. But we are losing. We are losing badly. We have lost our sense of who we are because we have lost our sense of whose we are.

We have become unknown—silent, faceless, nameless men—all for the sake of making sure that she doesn't get mad at us.

Do you not know that those who run in a race all run, but only one receives the prize? Run in such a way that you may obtain it.

1 CORINTHIANS 9:24 (NKJV)

LET YOUR "YES" BE "YES"

When we have a hard time saying "no" to others, we suffer two major consequences:

1. Our lives become unmanageable.
2. Our "yes" is not genuine, and we live less intimate lives.

We must be able to set limits with others if we are to maintain true harmony and intimacy with others. It's interesting that we believe doing the opposite will bring the same results. This is simply not true. Only when we set limits will our lives become more tractable again.

Keeping the peace never brings peace.

When I play the game of people pleasing, I might be saying "yes" on the outside, but the inside is another matter. It may be hard to believe that our friends and family want anything more than our compliance, but they do. They really do. They want our heart. When we have the courage to say "no", our "yes" becomes more genuine and wholehearted. Passivity convinces us that honesty and integrity should be sacrificed for the greater good of serving others. Making sure everyone's happy is what really matters, it argues. Actually, we're trying to ensure that everyone is happy with us. What a sad way to live. The opposite of Jesus' example. Jesus never bothered with winning man's approval. He was all about pleasing His Father.

And He who sent Me is with Me. The Father has not left Me alone, for I always do those things that please Him.

JOHN 8:29 (NKJV)

Jesus was mocked, scorned, even spit on simply because he stood for the truth and was straightforward with people. Jesus found his strength in knowing His Father was with Him. We also find the strength to avoid the peril of passivity when we understand on a fundamental level that we are not alone—our Father is always with us. When we are passive, we focus on—and become obsessed with—pleasing others, all because we fear their disapproval. When we act out of an understanding of who we are as fathered men, we act out of love and passion towards others because we know our Father loves and accepts us, no matter what others say about us.

Being passive might seem like an act of indifference. But actually, passivity is a choice—a choice to be unwilling to change for fear of the unknown. To break the power of passivity a man must give himself over to willingness.

THE BROTHERING
INTERACTIVE STUDY QUESTIONS

1. In what ways did you observe passivity in your family of origin (father, uncles, etc.)?

2. How has your passivity interfered in your relationship with your spouse or significant other?

3. How has your passivity interfered with your career/job or ministry?

4. How has your passivity interfered with your relationship with God?

5. Does your picture of God include any aspects of passivity?

6. If you could, what steps would you take to be less passive in your life?

THE FATHERING

My son,
Come to me, and allow me to remove your passivity.
This is not who you are, my son.
You are not a passive man.
You have allowed fear to guide you.
Fear of what others think of you.
That fear has told you to just do whatever people want
you to do.
Don't be troubled if someone isn't pleased with you.
Though I may not always be pleased with your choices,
I am still pleased with you.
I have created you, my son.
Let this be enough for you.

I love you.
Dad

A SON'S PRAYER

Father,

Thanks for creating the man that I truly am.

It's hard for me to see that man in me sometimes.

I have allowed fear to paint a different picture.

Fear has told me to make sure everyone is happy with me.

That I am only acceptable when others are happy with me.

And that it isn't enough that you are pleased with me.

Forgive me, Father.

Thank you that you are enough for me.

Give me courage to be direct with others.

Give me the courage to say "no" when I need to, so that my "yes" will truly be "yes".

Thank you for setting an example for me.

Thank you that I'm not a passive man at heart.

Help me to see the man you see in me.

I love you, Dad.

Amen

THE RESCUE

CHAPTER 6
THE WILLING MAN

If you are willing and obedient, you shall eat the good of the land.

ISAIAH 1:19 (NKJV)

THE second day of Base Camp, I went on a short hike with one of the guys I was rooming with. We were admiring the beauty of the sheer rock faces all around us when there in the stillness—out of nowhere—a question popped into to my mind.

"Are you willing?"

"Am I willing to what?" Not having a clue as to what He meant.

"Are you willing, son?" God repeated. "It all starts with willingness."

THE ULTIMATE PREREQUISITE

At the time, I wasn't sure what God was trying to tell me. Was this another primer? As I reflect on it now, it's obvious God was preparing me for something. But it was more than that. God wanted me to understand what gives any primer its wings—willingness.

Are you willing?

When God first posed the question, I heard it in the context of my willingness to do something. I didn't understand that God wanted me to experience something. The only doing part was the willingness itself.

God, what do you want me to do?

This is often the question we ask when trying to discern God's will—what do you want me to do? We are obsessed with activity. Doing makes us feel productive and in control. Yet, ironically, the more obsessed we are with doing, the more unmanageable our lives become. But what if God's will had nothing to do with our doing anything? What if it was never about what we could do? Perhaps we need to ask a different question.

Father, how do you want me to experience your fathering?

This question illuminates the place where willingness gives us freedom. When we're willing to let God father us, we shift our focus from doing something to experiencing someone—God the Father.

But now, O Lord, You are our Father, We are the clay, and You our potter; And all of us are the work of Your hand.

ISAIAH 64:8 (NASB)

A CHILDLIKE WILLINGNESS

"Hey buddy, can you hand me that little screwdriver?" a father asks his four year-old son.

The boy holds up a screwdriver. "You mean this one, Dad?"

"Yep. That's the one."

"Do you need the hammer, too, Dad?"

"Yeah, I think I do. Boy! You sure are good at picking out tools for me."

"Thanks." The boy grins, as he returns to *repairing* his tricycle. "Love you, Dad."

"I love you too, son."

———————————— · ————————————

When a little boy plays on the garage floor while his dad works on the family car, does he really care that much about Dad's plan or agenda? No. He just wants to be with his dad and help him fix the car. We can learn a lot from the willingness of a child. Like the dad in this story, God isn't all that concerned about our abilities. He cares only about our willingness and desire to be with Him. He doesn't need us to be able, just willing. He alone is able.

Now all glory to God, who is able to keep you from falling away and will bring you with great joy into his glorious presence without a single fault.

JUDE 1:24 (NLT)

No matter how much we think we've prepared ourselves for what may be coming next in life, we will always encounter another random event that we didn't consider. We can be more prepared, but never fully prepared. All we can be is willing.

We seldom do anything to the best of our ability; we do it to the best of our willingness (5).

—AUTHOR UNKNOWN

TAKING THE PLUNGE

Through the years in my practice, I've talked to many men who've told me they wanted to forgive someone, but they just weren't ready. What they usually meant by "not ready" was not willing. If we truly want to see change in our lives, we must go beyond just wanting it. Change occurs only when we're willing—willing to do whatever is necessary, ready or not.

For if there is first a willing mind, it is accepted according to what one has, and not according to what he does not have.

2 CORINTHIANS 8:12 (NKJV)

For years, I desired to connect with others on a deeper level, but I was unwilling to put myself out there and let God father me out of isolation. I had embraced doing life as a Lone Ranger, unwilling to cultivate a vulnerable and intimate relationship with the Father and others. Passivity ruled to the point where I couldn't bear the thought of putting forth so much effort. It seemed easier to coast along the way I had been.

When I arrived at Base Camp, I had begun to move from wanting to willing. My willingness proved critical for God to move in my life. When we choose to be willing, we go from spectator to participant, and we begin to see life in a whole new way. I love the following scripture in Mark illustrating how Jesus involved the will of a blind man in receiving his sight.

And Jesus answered and said to him, "What will you that I should do to you?" The blind man said to him, "Lord, that I might receive my sight".

MARK 10:51 (AKJV)

We are all blind in one way or another. Without being given new eyes to see, we remain buried in our rubble unaware of our predicament. All He asks of us is willingness.

Are you willing, son?

Before we are courageous. Before we are passionate. Before we are brothered. Before we are fathered. Before we are rescued. Before we are even vulnerable. We must be one thing.

Willing.

THE BROTHERING
INTERACTIVE STUDY QUESTIONS

1. What other words come to mind when you think of the word "willing"?

2. Describe a time when you were willing to do something you hadn't been willing to do before?

3. How did that willingness impact the quality of your life? (Referring to previous question)

4. How willing are you to let God lead you? What influences your willingness (childhood, relationships, fear, insecurity, etc.)?

5. Are there areas in your life (relationships, career, ministry, etc.) where you resist a willing attitude?

6. In what areas of your life are you willing to let God father you more? Take some time to pray with your brother(s) and invite your Father into these areas. Take time to process this experience with your brother(s).

THE FATHERING

My son,
Come to me and let me give you courage.
Courage to be willing.
Be willing to let me help you, son.
I want you to join me on this great adventure.
I have great plans for us, my son.
Don't let fear of the unknown rob you of all that
I have for you.
Bring your fears and confusion to me.
Are you willing to trust me?
Are you willing to believe I have good things for you,
no matter what comes your way?
Are you willing to let me father you, son?
Experience my fathering as you let go of trying to
control your life.
I will give you what you need.
Are you willing, son?

I love you.
Dad

A SON'S PRAYER

Dad,

I ask for courage to pray this prayer.

I am so derailed by my _____ (fears, isolation, passivity, busyness, etc.).

Please forgive me.

I invite you into every activity, every moment of my life.

I'm willing, Dad.

I invite your fathering into the areas of my life I've tried to control.

I'm willing.

I know that you will do your work in me and through me when I let you father me.

I'm willing, Father. Here I am.

I love you, Dad.

Amen

THE RESCUE

CHAPTER 7
THE VULNERABLE MAN

And He said to me, "My grace is sufficient for you, for my strength is made perfect in weakness."

2 CORINTHIANS 12:9 (AKJV)

ONE November a few years back, I went out for a run. As I finished, I started to feel pain in my lower right abdomen. I disregarded it, thinking it was just a pulled muscle.

No big deal.

Four weeks later, I sat in my surgeon's office and listened to the hapless diagnosis—sports hernia—though he couldn't be certain because this type of hernia doesn't always show up on an MRI.

Great.

I decided to go ahead with the surgery. The day of my operation, I felt nervous, anxious and completely vulnerable. The hospital staff didn't make it any easier when they went over the risks of general anesthesia right before they wheeled me over to the OR. Add to that the fact that tubes were inserted into virtually every orifice of my body.

Nice.

The surgeon told me he would insert a double mesh into my abdominal wall, and, assuming there were no complications during surgery, I'd be free to go home afterward.

As I woke from anesthesia, the operating room seemed empty. Still lying on the OR bed completely naked, I could feel cool air from the outside hallway. Then I noticed a shy, diminutive hospital aide standing there ready to help me into a seated position. She gave me a faint smile as she worked silently. She did not appear to speak English. This eliminated any chance for awkward small talk, for which I was grateful considering the fact that this complete stranger was now helping me put on my underwear and then the rest of my clothing. I did my best to assist her but was not much help. She was gentle with me. I tried to muster up a "thank you", but my vocal chords didn't cooperate, due to the trauma from being intubated during surgery. The aide said nothing, just smiled as she motioned for me to take a seat in the wheelchair. In protest, I stood to walk, but I quickly realized the futility of that endeavor as she helped me back into the wheelchair.

As if my pride hadn't taken a few hits already, the aide slowly wheeled me down a long hallway that wound its way to the other side of the building. We made it to the west entrance door where my wife was waiting in the car. I passed other patients and their families along the way as pride and shame took turns delivering blows.

You look like an idiot.
Doesn't this woman know you run marathons? Tell her to speed it up!
Do you realize how prideful you are?

When we arrived at the door, I tried to stand, assuming I would need to take it from there. She firmly but carefully redirected me back into the wheelchair and then pushed me out into the cold autumn air. It became quite clear that I had a long recovery ahead of me. Not just a few days. Not just a few weeks. But months.

As I got into the car, my sweet wife did her best to encourage her very crabby husband. "Honey, it'll be ok."

"Yup." I stared out the window.

"Do you want to talk about it?"

"Nope." I felt weak and exposed. I felt pissed off, and no one, not even Wendy, was going to talk me out of it.

Just get back to full strength and put this whole thing behind me.

Though it appeared more like a curse at the time, my hernia actually offered me a gift—the blessing of vulnerability.

RAW EXPOSURE VS. VULNERABILITY

Raw exposure happens when our expression of feelings and needs is met with judgment, shame or rejection. This result discourages us from being transparent with others in the future. Conversely, when our transparency with others is met with compassion and understanding, we experience healthy vulnerability. As we allow vulnerability and its healing impact into our experience, we no longer sidestep it—we pursue it.

"Judge not, that you be not judged. For with what judgment you judge, you will be judged; and with the measure you use, it will be measured back to you. And why do you look at the speck in your brother's eye, but do not consider the plank in your own eye? Or how can you say to your brother, 'Let me remove the speck from your eye'; and look, a plank is in your own eye?"

MATTHEW 7:1-4 (NKJV)

Being vulnerable with others is something I've avoided most of my life. There were times during childhood when I felt sad and lonely, but instead of going to my parents for support, I often made up an excuse and told them I was tired when they noticed I wasn't myself. Holed up in my room, I was afraid to tell them the truth for fear of looking weak and "acting like a baby". Expressing sadness to others became a crime in my mind, and the self-imposed punishment was solitary confinement. Isn't this what most men do when they encounter heavy emotions—repress them, withdraw or isolate? If I had a dollar for every time a man apologized to me for crying during a therapy session, I'd be a wealthy man. We are programmed to hide our feelings from an early age. We grow up in a society where sharing our emotions is eschewed.

Big boys don't cry. Man up. Don't be a wimp. Take it like a man.

Perhaps we need to rethink what it means to be a real man.

A REAL MAN

To share your weakness is to make yourself vulnerable; to make yourself vulnerable is to show your strength (6).

—CRISS JAMI

I have witnessed men taking the risk of being vulnerable in the company of other brothers, and I must say, there's not a ballsier move. A real man is willing to be vulnerable because he understands his survival as a real man depends on it. A real man is ready to be more honest with himself and others because he knows the pretending and posing is sucking the life out of his soul. A real man is a man who's willing to be real. Period. When we are known and loved for who we are, we are transformed. We become the real men Father God intended us to be. This cannot happen without being vulnerable with others. And it starts with prayer.

BEING DIRECT WITH GOD

God desires to help us find brothers who will walk with us on the journey. But the Prince of Darkness will do everything in his power to keep us from connecting with those brothers because it's through our brothers that God brings a key aspect of His fathering. Remember to pray. I know this sounds like I'm stating the obvious, but in the midst of our struggle, God is always trustworthy to meet our needs. He will provide brothers to walk with us if we ask.

Don't bargain with God. Be direct. Ask for what you need.

MATTHEW 7:7 (MSG)

About three weeks before Base Camp, one of the leaders sent out the following email. In it, he encouraged all the attendees to do something, which, at the time, felt incredibly vulnerable for me to consider.

John Hard
To: Base Camp Attendees
Re: Base Camp Weekend

Hey Guys,

Our gathering is only about 4 weeks away. We believe God is going to do something special. I hope you are getting as excited about our fall gathering in Colorado as I am.

I keep getting a sense that God is up to something a little weightier than just numbers. I think it's more than just a wish in my heart; I sense he really does have something huge in mind for each of us. I'm praying that will be the case.

I want to encourage you to begin now (if you haven't already) asking God to prepare your heart for all that he has for you during our time together.

Then, add this prayer question to your times with God: What if the Father asked you what you most wanted from him that weekend? How would you respond?

I imagine he is more excited than we are. It's kind of like when I would buy gifts for my young children, and I could hardly wait until Christmas to see their faces light up. I know I enjoyed it more than they did.
In the same way I believe he is ecstatic over what he sees coming our way in September.

See you soon!

John

God was asking me to be vulnerable with Him and ask for a gift. So I prayed this prayer:

Father, I ask that you bring me a brother to walk with on this journey. My faith is weak right now. Help me to trust you.

God understands how it feels to be vulnerable—more than we will ever know.

THE VULNERABLE GOD

When we ponder the attributes of God, we usually think in terms of strength and power, not vulnerability and weakness. To consider vulnerability and God in the same sentence seems oxymoronic. We have a hard time reconciling the two. How can the God of the universe be anything but powerful? After all, God wouldn't put Himself in a position of vulnerability. Right?

Wrong. Jesus did.

The King of Kings and the Lord of Lords came to earth as a baby. It doesn't get any more vulnerable than that. Well, actually it does. Jesus hung on a cross for the sins of all mankind. Doesn't fit the superhero mold, does it? Then again, Jesus never fit into anyone's mold.

He was a real man.

Think of yourselves the way Christ Jesus thought of himself. He had equal status with God but didn't think so much of himself that he had to cling to the advantages of that status no matter what. Not at all. When the time came, he set aside the privileges of deity and took on the status of a slave, became human! Having become human, he stayed human. It was an incredibly humbling process. He didn't claim special privileges. Instead, he lived a selfless, obedient life and then died a selfless, obedient death—and the worst kind of death at that—a crucifixion.

PHILIPPIANS 2:5-8 (MSG)

Time and time again, Jesus demonstrated his willingness to be vulnerable. As others walked away because they would not accept his teachings, Jesus turned to his twelve disciples and showed his need for their companionship.

At this point many of his disciples turned away and deserted him. Then Jesus turned to the Twelve and asked, "Are you also going to leave?"

JOHN 6:66-67 (NLT)

Here, in the book of Matthew, he expresses a need for the disciples' companionship again the night before he was crucified.

Then Jesus went with them to the olive grove called Gethsemane, and he said, "Sit here while I go over there to pray." He took Peter and Zebedee's two sons, James and John, and he became anguished and distressed. He told them, "My soul is crushed with grief to the point of death. Stay here and keep watch with me."

MATTHEW 26:36-38 (NLT)

We'd be hard pressed to find a better example of vulnerability than when Jesus expressed his sadness and sense of abandonment right before his death on the cross.

At about three o'clock, Jesus called out with a loud voice, "Eli, Eli, lema sabachthani?" which means "My God, my God, why have you abandoned me?"

MATTHEW 27:46 (NLT)

Jesus modeled for us how to pray. He modeled vulnerability and candor with His Father. He shows us it's not about saying all the right words—it's about saying what's on our heart.

As you have found in previous chapters, I've included some scripted prayers at the end of this chapter. These will help you be more vulnerable with God. These are not meant to be a "how to" kind of thing. These are just examples. It's all about the heart. When you speak to God, let your heart do the talking, Father God is listening.

For when we are vulnerable we can be rescued.

THE BROTHERING
INTERACTIVE STUDY QUESTIONS

1. What inhibits you from being more transparent with others (shame, fear of looking weak, fear of rejection, etc.)?

2. Describe a previous experience when you tried to be vulnerable but it turned out feeling like raw exposure.

3. With whom are you the most vulnerable? Why?

4. With whom would you like to be more vulnerable? Why?

5. How often are you vulnerable with God? Why or why not?

6. What would you like to tell Father God, if you felt free to be more vulnerable?

THE FATHERING

My son,
You're not alone in this struggle.
I know you need others to walk with you.
Come to me. Ask for what you need.
I will provide brothers to walk with you on your journey.
Remember not to judge your brothers when they
share with you.
Love them as I do.
Be quick to listen and slow to speak.
Let your words be kind and validating.
I want to hear what's really going on in your life.
I love it when you share your heart with me.
When you shut me out, it saddens me.
Don't worry about how to say it. Just say what's on
your heart, son.
No matter what you share with me—remember—there's
nothing that you could say that would make me love you
any less.

I love you, son.
Dad

A SON'S PRAYER

Dad,
Expressing my true self isn't easy for me.
I have kept my heart guarded and walled off.
Please help me take down these walls.
I've gotten so good at shutting everyone out that I
don't even know what I feel sometimes.
I want to be more vulnerable with others, but a part
of me is terrified.
Please hear the cries and longings of my heart.
Help my heart to soften.
Thank you for what you did for me on the cross.
Thank you for being so vulnerable.
I realize letting you father me will require being
more vulnerable.
I don't want to travel through life alone.
Give me the courage to put myself out there and meet
those you have placed on my path.
Give me the courage to be more vulnerable with others.
Help me to be more vulnerable with you.

I love you, Dad.
Amen

THE RESCUE

CHAPTER 8
THE RESCUED MAN

He will call upon Me and I will answer him; I will be with him in trouble; I will rescue him and honor him.

PSALM 91:15 (NASB)

BOOM! It sounded like a bomb went off. Bantum's vehicle shook violently as windows from some of the nearby buildings shattered, leaving shards of glass everywhere. Fear gripped him as he tried to steady himself.

C'mon, focus! You can do this!

John Bantum had only been on the job for nine days and during that time it was mainly uneventful. Now, on his first day off, he was being thrust into his first catastrophic scenario as an EMT. He remembered the words of one his instructors.

Time is of the essence. Every second counts.

He jumped out of his SUV and bolted in the direction of the blast, praying he wouldn't find any victims or casualties. But he knew the area well—it was densely populated. Civilians were most likely in the vicinity when the explosion occurred.

As he turned the corner, he saw it. Like a demolition crew had used a hundred wrecking balls all at once, there was debris everywhere. He could hear something. Beneath the rubble, someone was talking.

"Shit! I knew I should have kept Peyton Manning on my roster! Who knew he would have a flipping comeback this year!" The buried man lamented while looking at his phone as a gaping wound on the left side of his neck bled profusely.

"Dispatch, we have a man alive. I repeat, man alive!" Bantum yelled into his cellphone. "Sir, are you okay?"

"Yeah. Just lost my shorts this week, three grand to be exact. Now the wife is gonna pull the plug on my fantasy football because I was too much of a dumb-ass to stick with my instincts. She probably already knows I used the emergency fund. Damn it!"

Though Bantum's visual was largely obstructed, he could see that time was running out for the injured man. Still, he tried to keep his tone even and positive. "Keep talking to me, buddy. Just don't move. Okay?"

"Hey, wait a minute. Yes! I still have this weekend to recoup my cash and put the money back into the account! Sweet!"

"Sir, what's your name?" Bantum was trying to help the injured man stay focused.

But the man's voice began to weaken. "Who am I kidding...she always finds out...I'll get the money back, honey...I promise...please don't be mad...I'm sorry baby... so sorry...sorry." The man started slipping out of consciousness.

"Need backup now! Victim is losing consciousness! C'mon, buddy! Keep talkin' to me!"

Silence.

"I can't hear you! Keep talkin' to me! C'mon now, stay with me!"

Still no response.

"Sir, can you hear me?!"

No response.

What interferes most with a man's rescue is not the rubble in his life, but the denial that usually comes along with it. He simply doesn't believe he needs to be rescued. He gets lulled into a fog thinking he has it all under control, when—in reality—his life has become completely unmanageable. We've forgotten how desperately we need God and His fathering. Like the man in the rubble, we're losing consciousness, and we don't even know it. What will we do when the hand of rescue comes?

THE DANGER OF PLAYING IT SAFE

In The Monuments Men, a powerful film directed by George Clooney, James Granger leads a group of men on a rescue mission (7). The world's finest works of art have been pilfered by the Nazis during World War II and it's up to Granger and his men to find the stolen treasures. While searching an abandoned coal mine, Granger accidentally steps on a land mine. Realizing immediately that the smallest move will detonate the device, he weighs his options.

Apparently the precious works of art aren't the only ones needing rescue here.

Granger agonizes over his predicament and finally concludes it would be better for everyone if they just leave him behind to die. But his comrades won't have any of it. They deny his request and figure out a way to counterbalance his weight so he can step off the explosive without blowing them all to bits.

Granger needed help, but he had given up all hope for rescue. He was resigned to standing on that bomb for the rest of his life. During one of the Base Camp sessions, the leaders showed this movie clip. Of course, this was no coincidence.

Another primer.

How often does our fear of change immobilize us and convince us that we're better off staying put? We become stuck. Stuck in our jobs. Stuck in our dysfunctional relationships. Stuck in our addictions. Stuck. Fear often gives us the same counsel it gave James Granger:

Whatever you do…don't move.

So, we live frozen lives. We stay with the status quo because it seems safe. And herein lies a dangerous and sometimes even fatal lie.

Nobody gets hurt if you play it safe.

During the months leading up to Base Camp, I had resigned myself to a frozen life. Only, I didn't call it that at the time. I referred to it as *being smart about my decisions.* I had fallen for my own euphemistic rhetoric. There was nothing smart about it. I was playing it safe, and it was killing me. I was dying inside, but that didn't matter as long as I was paying the bills and doing a job that contributed to the benefit of society, I reasoned. Like James Granger, I told everyone to go on ahead without me while I waited to die. I had given up on my heart simply because I didn't want to be a burden. How long was Granger going to stand there until he started to get a little bit tired? How long until he made that fatal misstep and blew himself to smithereens? I, too, was getting tired. So weary. But, like Granger, I pressed on, willing myself to keep standing. Just a little longer.

Granger had a choice to make. Either accept help or die alone. Similarly, this is what happens to our hearts when we don't accept rescue from others; we die a slow and lonely death. Due to nothing more than fear of looking weak.

THE VILIFICATION OF WEAKNESS

Weakness—our arch nemesis. So we think. As we learned in a previous chapter, shame, not weakness, is the real culprit here. Shame puts a negative spin on weakness and thereby causes us to hide our weakness from others. This puts a huge roadblock in front of the first responders that God sends our way. If we are not willing to admit our weaknesses, we will not be rescued. Therefore it is critical that we come to an understanding. Weakness is not the problem—it's actually part of the solution.

Whether we acknowledge it or not, we are weak. When we let others know we are weak, it is no longer suppressed or kept secret. When we acknowledge our weakness before God and others, we begin to access His strength. Through the persistence of his brothers, Granger eventually let them into his weakness. What a great example of God's fathering through brothering.

And He said to me, "My grace is sufficient for you, for My strength is made perfect in weakness." Therefore most gladly I will rather boast in my infirmities, that the power of Christ may rest upon me. Therefore I take pleasure in infirmities, in reproaches, in needs, in persecutions, in distresses, for Christ's sake. For when I am weak, then I am strong.

2 CORINTHIANS 12:9-10 (NKJV)

As we rescue one another, we do so not with our own strength, but with the strength of our Father. What a powerful picture of Father God's hand coming down through us as we reach out to a brother buried beneath the rubble.

THE USUAL SUSPECTS

Of the hundreds of patients I've interviewed in sessions over the past 25 years, when it comes to the rubble in a man's life, these are the usual suspects: fatherlessness, isolation, passivity, addiction, and shame.

More specifically:

- Feeling distant from God because of a distorted picture of God as Father.

- Isolating from others in order to avoid being vulnerable and looking weak.
- Depending on work performance for a sense of worth and self-identity.
- Resorting to passivity to avoid conflict with others, especially with spouse or significant other.
- Struggling with addictive behavior to numb loneliness and shame.
- Resigning to living in survival mode and abandoning what makes the heart passionate.

It is likely you will identify with one or more of these examples. It may be difficult to imagine life without the rubble. It can feel hopeless—like there's no way out of the wreckage. Well, there is hope. There most certainly is. Our Father knew we desperately needed His intervention. This is why he sent his Son to rescue us.

THE ULTIMATE RESCUE

There can be no better example of rescue than the one demonstrated by Christ on the cross. Jesus reached down— way down—into our rubble.

"When he ascended to the heights, he led a crowd of captives and gave gifts to his people." Notice that it says, "He ascended." This clearly means that Christ also descended to our lowly world.

And the same one who descended is the one who ascended higher than all the heavens, so that he might fill the entire universe with himself.

EPHESIANS 4:8-10 (NLT)

Jesus' death on the cross paid the penalty for the sins of every person who has lived and will ever live. The level of suffering He underwent is unimaginable. He did this so that we would be rescued from the rubble of our sin.

But he was pierced for our rebellion, crushed for our sins. He was beaten so we could be whole. He was whipped so we could be healed.

ISAIAH 53:5 (NLT)

He did this so that we could become sons of God. No longer separated from Him by our sin. Jesus came to earth to unite us with our Father. We have access to Father God through the rescuing work done by Jesus on the cross.

Jesus told him, "I am the way, the truth, and the life. No one can come to the Father except through me."

JOHN 14:6 (NLT)

THE OUTSTRETCHED HAND

There will be rubble in this life. It is unavoidable. The question is—will you allow yourself to be rescued from it? If we're going to be pulled out of the rubble, we must let others know we're in the rubble. This involves taking some inventory of the usual suspects in our lives. We all need to be rescued and it's not some one-time experience where we are good to go from then on. No. We will need to be rescued from time to time throughout our lives.

Guard your heart above all else, for it determines the course of your life.

PROVERBS 4:23 (NLT)

A willingness to be vulnerable is necessary if we are to be used by God to rescue another. It took a considerable amount of vulnerability for those men to stay with Granger as long as it took, even if it meant risking their own lives in the process.

This is where the new chapter of our lives begins if we allow ourselves to be rescued.

THE BROTHERING
INTERACTIVE STUDY QUESTIONS

1. In what ways can you relate to James Granger in the scene from The Monuments Men described in this chapter?

2. How typical is it for you to ask for help? What does it feel like right now to say the words "I need help"?

3. How are you currently playing it safe, and how might that course of action be dangerous for you?

4. Explore the examples of rubble listed in this chapter. Which ones can you relate to most? Why?

5. Describe a time when someone rescued you.

6. Describe a time when you were part of a rescue mission in someone else's life?

7. What do you need God to rescue you from? Ask Him to show you a picture of His rescue. Share this experience with your brother(s).

THE FATHERING

My son,

I've watched you struggle so much in this life.

I have been trying to rescue you for so long.

Many times I called out, but you did not hear my voice.

Many times I reached out to you, but you did not
take my hand.

This grieved me, son.

Reach out now, and be vulnerable with me.

Let me pull you from the wreckage.

Let me free you from the rubble in your life.

It's my desire to rescue all men.

You are worth all the suffering that my Son went
through to rescue you.

I will put brothers on your path to walk along side of you.

Please don't turn them away.

For they are an extension of my hand reaching out to you.

I love you, son.

Dad

A SON'S PRAYER

Dad,

I come to you.

I hold out my hand to you.

Please hear my cry.

Thank you for your patience with me.

I'm so sorry that my unwillingness to ask for help
has grieved you so.

Father, please forgive me.

Thank you that you searched relentlessly for me
through the rubble.

Thank you that I am worth more than many sparrows to you.

I now confess my rubble to you, Father (resignation,
addictions, isolation, passivity, fear, etc.).

Please begin to free me from this rubble.

I accept the rescuing work that Jesus did on the cross to save
me—to bring me freedom and peace.

All those times when you reached out to me and I didn't reach
back—you could have given up on me, but you didn't, Dad.

You never gave up on me.

I love you.

Amen

THE REDEMPTION

CHAPTER 9
THE PASSIONATE MAN

Delight yourself also in the LORD, and He shall give you the desires of your heart.

PSALM 37:4 (NKJV)

TWO weeks after I got back from Base Camp, a friend of mine asked me to read the manuscript of a book he was working on. One of the chapters described the impact his father's death had had on his life. After reading this, something rather unexpected happened.

I started writing my own story.

Before I knew it, I had opened a blank document and was typing away as fast as I could. *What am I doing?* I felt this strange assortment of emotions ranging from bemusement to excitement. Then it got even stranger. Some days I started early in the morning and wrote until I had to go to work. Other days I came home after work and wrote late into the night. It got to the point where I was writing upwards of 40 hours or more a week.

During much of that time, I battled with doubt about my abilities as a writer. One day I had a candid conversation with God about it.

"Father, who am I kidding? I can't do this. After all, it's not like I'm a real author."

"You can do this." God said.

"I'm not so sure."

"I am, son."

"How can you be?"

"Because you have the same gift I gave to your father."

My heart stopped.

And then two words came to mind—Grape Crush.

THE LEGACY

My father was the editor of a small-town newspaper where I grew up. It was not uncommon for me to visit him at his office especially during summer months when boredom would often set in. I can recall hearing the sound of heavy machinery and the smell of ink as the giant printing press worked its magic. As a boy, I had no idea what an editor did. All I cared about was that bottle of Grape Crush I got to pull out of the old pop machine. On a hot summer day nothing tasted better.

I still have a few newspaper clippings of some of the articles my father wrote. He was a talented man, but his craft never inspired any emulation on my part. Of course, there was good reason for that. All those years of hating him caused me to avoid taking any path that resembled his. Whatever he was, I was bound and determined not to be—end of story.

My middle name is Paul, which was my father's name. Throughout much of my life, whenever I had to provide my signature, like many people do, I just abbreviated it with its first initial. I always thought it was just easier that way. Though in retrospect, the brevity of my signature wasn't just a matter of convenience. It was really about the hatred I had harbored all those years. It just goes to show how pervasive hatred and resentment can be—even affecting one's own signature. Never using my full middle name was another way of excluding my father from my life.

But God had something else in mind.

He asked that I embrace the identity He gave me as His son. An identity that included the legacy of my earthly father. After all, I am not just my Father's son. I am also my *father's* son. Unfortunately, my father's legacy wasn't solely comprised of gifts or talents. No, his legacy also included the impact of his woundedness. But praise God! We have a redeemer! He takes what the Prince of Darkness meant for evil and turns it into something good. Something very good. This is what makes any legacy a *gift* to the next generation because if we allow Him to, God will most certainly redeem it.

My father's passion for writing is a significant part of the legacy he left me. But he also left me something even more significant. Something I can be just as passionate about—my name. When I write my full signature now, it makes me think of what Father God has restored and redeemed in my life.

So I will restore to you the years that the swarming locust has eaten, the crawling locust, the consuming locust, and the chewing locust, my great army, which I sent among you. You shall eat in plenty and be satisfied, and praise the name of the Lord your God, who has dealt wondrously with you; and My people shall never be put to shame.

JOEL 2:25-26 (NKJV)

LIKE FATHER, LIKE SON

Living passionately does not happen by chance. Nor does it occur by an act of our will—we cannot will passion. It goes beyond talent or knowing what makes us come alive. Passion is a way of being—a natural result of being fathered by God because God is inherently passionate. Being passionate originates in His DNA.

You must not bow down to another god, because the LORD is passionate: the LORD's name means "a passionate God."

EXODUS 34:14 (CEB)

I never expected to write a book. Never wanted to. I always hated writing in school and thought I was a miserable failure at it. When I started writing last year, I did so only because I felt compelled. Something had gotten ahold of me, and it wouldn't let go. But it wasn't just *something*, it was someone—Father

God. He was compelling me through the vehicle of writing to express His love for others and me. His love—not the writing—was the source and essence of the passion I felt every time I sat down to write. This is a critical distinction to make when we try and navigate the path of passion. If we're not careful, we can get swept up into a love affair with our passions and lose sight of the one who gave them to us. Passion does not call us.

God does.

THE PLIGHT OF PASSION

When we live our lives with passion, we will likely have a battle on our hands. The Prince of Darkness does not want us to live as passionate men. Not because he is threatened by our passions, but because he is threatened by what makes our passions effective and impactful—God and His fathering. I'm sure Satan would love nothing more than for me to become distracted with writing a bestseller so I miss out on God's fathering through the passion of writing. How easy it is for us to become sidetracked and miss the point of why God gives us our passions in the first place.

But if I say I'll never mention the Lord or speak in his name, his word burns in my heart like a fire. It's like a fire in my bones! I am worn out trying to hold it in! I can't do it!

JEREMIAH 20:9 (NLT)

Jeremiah has a *fire in his bones. He must speak.* He just cannot hold it in any longer. Some might interpret this to mean that we should pursue whatever it is that truly compels us. But there's more to it than that. Look at what he says in the beginning of the verse: *But if I say I'll never mention the Lord or speak in his name, his word burns in my heart like a fire.*

Jeremiah's real passion was not public speaking. Was he good at it? Maybe. Did it make him come alive? Perhaps. But what is certain is Jeremiah's deepest passion—the Lord God.

Hobbies, careers, material possessions, relationships, sports— regardless of what it is—our passions will run our lives if we don't place them under the headship of God's fathering. Contrarily, when we allow God to father our passions, we realize their true relevance in the context of God's plan for our lives. The key to a passionate life involves letting God father our passions lest we end up like a ship without a rudder.

Look also at ships: although they are so large and are driven by fierce winds, they are turned by a very small rudder wherever the pilot desires.

JAMES 3:4 (NKJV)

THE PASSIONATE HUSBAND

When we experience the fathering of God through the brothering of men, we enter the process of becoming the men God created us to be. Doing so can have a profound impact on our marriage. We're freer to love our wives out of wholeness as men fathered by God. One of the main reasons we can operate out of passion and not out of fear is because we no longer choose to find our identity in our wife's approval.

We change our mindset because we experience an intimate relationship with our Father who affirms our true identity as His sons. Otherwise, fear pulls us back into the *Addiction Cycle* (previously discussed in The Addicted Man chapter and again shown below).

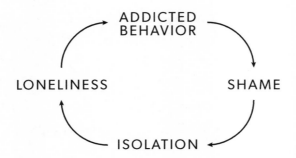

There is no fear in love; but perfect love casts out fear, because fear involves torment. But he who fears has not been made perfect in love.

1 JOHN 4:18 (NKJV)

PASSIONATE SEX

When we choose to operate out of love and not fear, we end up loving our spouse with more passion. Sex is no exception. Sex becomes a connective experience going well beyond physical pleasure—it becomes intimate. Intimate sex might sound redundant, but it is not. The more we give ourselves to our spouse—heart, mind, spirit and body—the more intimate and satisfying sex becomes. But if we limit our connectivity to a physical level only, we not only short-change the intimacy, we short-change the sex.

Like every other area of our lives, our sex life needs God's fathering. Take time to stop and pray beforehand. This honors God, as well as our spouse. If you have never done this before, it might feel awkward and like a total vibe-kill, but it won't be. Ask for Father God's blessing, guidance and protection over your time together with your wife. It actually makes a noticeable difference.

THE PASSIONATE FATHER

Dick Hoyt offers us a great example of passion. His son, Rick, has been confined to a wheelchair all of his life due to having Cerebral Palsy since birth. But that devastating disease has been no match for Dick's love for his son. Together, they have finished 1,091 sporting events, including 252 triathlons, 70 marathons, 94 half-marathons, and 155 five-kilometer races (8).

Dick Hoyt's passion goes deeper than just running triathlons. His passion is really about his son and the new adventure they experience together every time they enter another race.

When we experience God's fathering, we discover the journey of passion. This is the greatest adventure we will ever know. We partner with our Father as we travel down the trail letting Him set the agenda. It goes beyond the destination. It brings energy and purpose to every area of our lives.

And the LORD went before them by day in a pillar of cloud to lead the way, and by night in a pillar of fire to give them light, so as to go by day and night.

EXODUS 13:21 (NKJV)

THE BROTHERING
INTERACTIVE STUDY QUESTIONS

1. What are you passionate about?

2. What has gotten in the way of your passions and kept you from leading a more passionate life?

3. In what ways has your father passed on his legacy to you (positively)?

4. If you could be utterly fearless for one moment, in what way(s) would you show your spouse or significant other more passion?

5. What does it feel like to know that Father God is passionate about you?

6. Take time to pray and ask God about the next adventure He wants you to join Him on. Ask Him to show you a picture of what it might look like. Share what you notice with your brothers(s).

THE FATHERING

My son,

I have put my desires in your heart, but the evil one wants to rob you of the joy I have for you.

Keep your eyes on me, and I will keep you safe.

I created you, and I created your passions.

Remember, it is I who gives your passions direction and meaning.

Without me, passion will either fizzle out or control you.

Don't mistake the gift for the giver, my son.

I am the creator of all things. Every good and perfect gift comes from me.

I care so deeply about your heart.

I will show you more as we walk this path together.

I have many adventures for us to experience.

I love spending time with you.

I love you, son.

Dad

A SON'S PRAYER

Dad,

Please help me identify and understand the passions you have placed in my heart.

Show me how to enjoy the passions you've given me while keeping my eyes on you.

Please give me courage to pursue my relationship with

_____ with passion and without fear.

I am so glad you call me your son. This is my truest identity.

You are the giver of all the gifts in my life.

I worship you alone, Father.

Thank you for inviting me into this great adventure with you.

Let's ride together on this journey, shoulder to shoulder.

I love you, Dad.

Amen

THE REDEMPTION

CHAPTER 10
THE FATHERED MAN

A father to the fatherless, defender of widows—this is God, whose dwelling is holy.

PSALM 68:5 (NLT)

I'M in the front row of an empty theater sitting next to a little boy who can't be more than five years old. He looks a lot like me, and then I realize—he is me. A lone spotlight shines on a man in his early thirties sitting in a chair in the middle of the stage. It dawns on me that it's Jesus. Jesus looks out at both of us, and then asks the boy to come to Him. I find it odd to watch my younger self walk up the steps and go over to where Jesus sits. Jesus turns and looks deep into the boy's eyes as He extends his arms to him.

Slowly the younger me climbs up onto His lap and says a word in the form of a question. "Daddy?"

"Yeah, buddy, that's right." Jesus smiles as tears begin to run down his face.

Then the boy leans back and lets Jesus hold him. He looks so peaceful sitting there with Jesus. They sit there for a while and then the picture fades.

I must have been half awake when this picture—a simple picture of God's fathering—came to me one morning. God was showing me what it looked like to trust him like a son. There was a paradigm shift occurring. I was beginning to see my need for God from the perspective of a son rather than a servant or follower. God was becoming the Dad I always needed.

Philip said to Him, "Lord, show us the Father, and it is sufficient for us." Jesus said to him, "Have I been with you so long, and yet you have not known Me, Philip? He who has seen Me has seen the Father; so how can you say, 'Show us the Father'? Do you not believe that I am in the Father, and the Father in Me? The words that I speak to you I do not speak on My own authority; but the Father who dwells in Me does the works. Believe Me that I am in the Father and the Father in Me, or else believe Me for the sake of the works themselves."

JOHN 14:8-11 (NKJV)

DAD ISSUES

We can travel the backwards journey working through the issues of our past and still not be sure where to go after that. I had worked through all my hatred for my earthly father, but I still struggled with trusting God as my Father. The process of allowing God's fathering into our lives is a lifelong journey. If we're honest, we would admit we hold onto the reins most of the time. It makes us feel so vulnerable to let go and let God have total control of our lives.

No thanks, God. I got this. I'll let you know if I need anything from you.

When we live fathered lives, we find true freedom. More freedom than all our self-reliance and self-preservation could ever offer. The more I give God control over my life, the freer I am. I am free because I don't have to make it all happen. I don't have to try to affect the outcome. I can just be the man

God designed me to be. He can take care of all the intangibles. Unfortunately, entrusting our will to God often doesn't occur on a day-to-day basis. This only happens when we start seeing a new image of God.

IN FATHER WE TRUST

As mentioned previously, self-reliance is something we learn at a young age to protect ourselves from the likes of shame, rejection and abandonment. As a boy, I knew my dad wasn't going to be the father I needed so I determined it was up to me to find my own way. And thus, I believed a horrible lie to protect my heart.

I really don't need a father.

Nothing could be further from the truth. Submitting our will to God and letting Him father our lives is an ongoing battle. Despite our confessions, we often still take matters into our own hands. How we picture God is critical in determining whether we will put our trust in Him or in our own ability to take care of ourselves.

For much of my life, I viewed God as distant. I imagined He felt disappointed in me because I didn't perform up to some standard. My dad's often voiced criticism of me played a role in distorting my image of Father God—no doubt, but what twisted the picture even more were, ironically, some of the messages I received in church. It wasn't always what was said, but what was not said. There was such an emphasis on *doing*. And if you weren't doing your part, God was disappointed in you. It was all about what I could do for Him—nothing more, nothing less.

THE WHO IS IN THE WHOSE

It wasn't until I started experiencing the fathering of God that I really began to understand one very important thing: God loved me no matter what I did or didn't do. And His acceptance and approval of me wasn't based on what I could do. It was based on whose I was. He loved me because I was His son. He called me "son" even when I made bad choices. His love for me didn't ebb and flow, like my behavior.

When I started experiencing God as a Father who loved me unconditionally, it drew me to Him and I wanted to give Him more control over my life. What man doesn't want to bring joy to his father when he believes his father adores him and just wants to be with him? When our picture of God starts to reflect a loving Father who is intensely proud of and crazy about his sons, we realize it isn't about our performance for Him—but rather, our relationship with Him. We start seeing God as a Father who loves and delights in us as the apple of His eye. This makes us want to be with Him and be like Him all the more.

He found him out in the wilderness, in an empty, windswept wasteland. He threw his arms around him, lavished attention on him, guarding him as the apple of his eye.

DEUTERONOMY 32:10 (MSG)

THE INTIMATE FATHER

God calls us into obedience through intimacy with Him that transforms our lives as His sons. Otherwise, we rely on our own strength.

I can do all things through Christ who strengthens me.

PHILIPPIANS 4:13 (NKJV)

When we embrace our sonship through Christ, we realize we, too, are dearly loved.

After his baptism, as Jesus came up out of the water, the heavens were opened and he saw the Spirit of God descending like a dove settling on him. And a voice from heaven said, "This is my dearly loved Son, who brings me great joy."

MATTHEW 3:16-17 (NLT)

How often had I previously failed to see the intimate language here? Imagine what this scripture would have sounded like coming from Corporate America sent in the form of a memo.

To all employees of Earth,

Please join me in welcoming our new Chief Executive Officer, Jesus Christ.

Sincerely,
God
Chairman of the Board

Instead, our Heavenly Father speaks in a loving, intimate way. He says something only a loving parent would say, "This is my dearly loved Son, who brings me great joy." How powerful it must have been for Jesus (who was not only fully God, but also fully man) to hear His Father say this. God is showing His character as a loving Father who isn't afraid to show His affection. This wasn't God just sending out a memo letting everyone know who the real Messiah was. This was a proud and loving Father publicly affirming His Son.

WORDS MATTER

We settle for a distant relationship with God because we find it difficult to conceptualize what intimacy actually looks like between Father God and ourselves. Providentially, scripture gives us the ultimate example of intimacy between a father and son—God the Father and Jesus the Son. Jesus was all about His Father. Never once in the New Testament did Jesus address His

Father as "God" when speaking to him. Not once. In fact, often He referred to God as "Abba (Daddy)". It can feel vulnerable to address God as "Abba, Daddy, or Dad". Yet, what is prayer if it's not vulnerable? What is connection with God if it's not intimate?

Words matter. They really do.

Sometimes when I pray, I use the word "Dad" because it challenges me to be more vulnerable and transparent. I've found that the more vulnerable I am during my prayer time, the more real and meaningful it becomes. It's surprising how using one word can make such a huge difference. It illuminates the true picture of God and mitigates our distorted ones. It helps us to see God as a passionate and pleased Father who we surrender our will to on a daily basis, not out of fear, but out of love. This is what being fathered is all about.

And because we are his sons, God sent the Spirit of his Son into our hearts, the Spirit who calls out, "Abba, Father".

GALATIANS 4:6 (NIV)

Here's another word that matters—son. When we think of God, do we hear him calling us "son"? The God of the universe calls us His sons. He really does. We have been grafted into sonship due to the work of Christ on the cross.

But we see Jesus, who was made a little lower than the angels, for the suffering of death crowned with glory and honor, that He, by the grace of God, might taste death for everyone. For it was fitting for Him, for whom are all things and by whom are all things, in bringing many sons to glory, to make the captain of their salvation perfect through sufferings.

HEBREWS 2:9-10 (NKJV)

THE FATHERED PATH

Being a fathered man doesn't mean we have achieved a level of perfection or exclusive standing in some sort of elite club. It just means we want to turn our lives over to God and let him father us every step of the journey, knowing full well it will be a process.

The disciples had plenty of their own rubble: pride, doubt, betrayal, and fear. They struggled just like we do, yet God still fathered them along the way. And they brought His fathering to many. What a great example of experiencing the fathering of God through the brothering of men. Though far from perfect, the disciples were willing to follow wherever He led them. The power of imperfection, indeed.

Simon Peter replied, "Lord, to whom would we go? You have the words that give eternal life."

JOHN 6:68 (NLT)

THE BROTHERING
INTERACTIVE STUDY QUESTIONS

1. What words, memories, or pictures do you associate with the word "father"?

2. Can you think of some past experiences that might have distorted your image of God as Father?

3. What do you notice when you invite Jesus into those distorted images or memories?

4. What is your picture of God when you imagine him as your Father, Dad, or Daddy?

5. In what ways do you need Father God to affirm you as a man?

6. In what areas of your life have you pushed away God's fathering?

7. In what specific areas of your life would you like to ask for more of God's fathering?

THE FATHERING

My son,
You bring me joy because I created you.
You are my son and I love being your Dad.
Bring your questions and your doubts to me.
Let me come into your struggles.
It's okay, son. I'm here with you.
Open the arms of your heart and receive the love
I have for you.
Let me father you, son, in all circumstances.
Tell me where you feel weakest, and let me be
your strength.
Let me show you who I truly am.
I have not abandoned you, son.
I'm not too busy to talk with you.
I'm here.
Let me show you the man you truly are.
The man I created you to be.

I love you, son.
Dad

FATHERING EXERCISE

Close your eyes and have another man read *Words from the Father* (page 133) to you. Then answer/discuss the following questions.

1. What was it like to hear these words spoken to you through another man?

2. What words stand out the most? What words make you uncomfortable? What words draw you in?

A SON'S PRAYER

Dad,
Thank you for your fathering.
I have needed it for a long time.
I was so unaware of how much I need it.
I have felt disconnected from you at times, Dad.
I have made the mistake of seeing you as a distant
or angry God.
I didn't see you as a loving Father I could be close to,
but rather, someone I must perform for.
I realize now how my experiences with others have
impacted my picture of you.
Forgive me for judging you, Father.
Forgive me for avoiding you.
I want to start a new chapter in my life with you as
my loving Father.
I open my heart to you today and ask for your fathering.
Please put brothers on my path who will bring your
fathering to me as well.
Thanks for loving me.

I love you, Dad.
Amen

THE REDEMPTION

CHAPTER 11
THE BROTHERED MAN

As iron sharpens iron so a man sharpens a friend.

PROVERBS 27:17 (NLT)

THROUGHOUT my time at Base Camp, God seemed to be drawing me deeper into His presence, but for much of the 3-day weekend, I scarcely noticed. My self-preservation had made a tactical error—it assumed I wouldn't be presented with any real opportunity to be vulnerable. I reasoned that most men weren't that interested in discussing anything beyond the superficial, and if the interaction did go deeper, it would likely focus on the cerebral and analytical. I really didn't see it coming, and before I knew it, there it was, right in front of me. I could hear my wife's words echoing in my head.

What if it's not what you expected? What if God blesses you with a gift?

A LEAP OF FAITH

The people who help us grow toward true self offer unconditional love, neither judging us to be deficient nor trying to force us to change but accepting us exactly as we are (9).

—PARKER PALMER

That afternoon I went rappelling with some of the guys. The rather humbling experience forced me to rely on the skill and expertise of our guide. Though just 20 years old, his gentle leadership taught me patience, humility and a healthy dependence on others and God. What a monumental experience to lean back into the rope, suspended 150 feet in the air with eight men cheering me on to take that first big step.

"C'mon, Tom. You got this."

This was more than camaraderie or some sort of team building exercise. The men who surrounded me fathered me, and I felt as though I could hear God speaking through them.

"C'mon, son, you can do this. I'm right here with you."

Another primer.

After I got back from rappelling, it was time for another session. I listened as men talked about how their passions had gotten lost in the hustle and bustle of their busy lives. As I listened to their stories, it became more apparent—I hadn't just lost my passion—I had lost me.

"Would anyone else like to take a couple of minutes to share?" one of the leaders asked.

Without even realizing it, my hand stuck straight up in the air. I felt a wave of emotion building. Like a tsunami less than a mile off shore, I could do nothing to stop it.

The leader glanced in my direction. "Go ahead."

"I'm Tom, and I'm a psychologist. I . . . help people."

Silence.

"I guess I've been doing that all my life. I grew up in a family where I thought it was my job to make sure everybody was okay. So then, of course, I chose a helping profession for a career."

More silence.

"Anyway, I'm pretty good at it. You know . . . helping people. What I'm not so good at is . . . letting others help me."

And there it was. Through all my rambling, I had made a discovery—I needed to let others help me. Such a basic truth that I'm sure it struck no one else in the room as profound. Except me. Tears started to roll down my face as I wiped them with the back of my hand.

"Thanks, Tom." The leader nodded at me.

The late afternoon session was over and now it was time for supper. I had taken off my mask and I felt incredibly exposed. The thought of sitting down and having to make small talk over dinner wasn't all that appealing, to say the least. All I wanted to do was head back to my room and isolate myself from everyone. But God was right there to redirect me.

"Just go to the dining hall, son." He said.

So I walked along with everyone else up the dirt path to the dining hall for supper, but as it turned out, spaghetti would have to wait.

A FELLOW TRAVELER

Standing in line, with my plate and fork, I stared straight ahead in a deliberate attempt to avoid making eye contact with anyone. Suddenly, I felt someone tap my shoulder.

"Hey Tom, could I talk to you for a second?" A guy I barely recognized from the group session earlier stood behind me.

I nodded. We made our way to the lobby outside the dining hall.

"You've got a good heart, Tom." He poked his index finger into the left side of my chest.

Who is this guy?

As if reading my mind, he stuck out his hand. "I'm Ralph." Before I had a chance to respond, he continued. "Tom, you and I are a lot alike. We reach out and help everybody else, but we don't let anybody help us. I've got a picture I want to show you."

He pulled out his cell phone and brought up a photo of a scene where three cowboys are riding together side by side. "The cowboy on the left appears to be looking away and off doing his own thing. The cowboy on the right is talking to the guy in the middle probably trying to help him with something. We don't like being the one in the middle much, do we? We feel more comfortable being the guy who is always helping."

I nodded.

"It's easier for us to try and help everybody else so we don't have to be vulnerable with anybody. Then no one has to know how much pain we're in."

I nodded again.

"Because we think if they saw how much damn pain we're in, they probably wouldn't stick around. Would they, Tom?"

"Probably not."

"Tom, do you want me to join you on your journey?"

"What did you say?" I narrowed my eyes involuntarily. What Ralph didn't know at the time was that I prayed for this very thing three weeks ago. I prayed for a brother to walk with me on my journey.

"I asked you if you wanted me to join you on your journey."

"Okay," I said quietly, still in disbelief.

"Well then ask me."

Did he just say, 'ask me'? "You want me to ask you?" I looked at him quizzically.

"Yep." Ralph nodded.

"Okay. All right. Ralph, will you join me on my journey?" This time I spoke with a bit more confidence.

"Yep." He smiled and nodded again.

At the time, I had no idea what this exchange would lead to, but I knew God was doing something significant through it. He wasn't just bringing me a new friend or brother. He was bringing His fathering to me through Ralph. Turns out, God wanted me to do the same for him. Through all this, God was helping Ralph and I get our hearts back. And a whole lot more.

If a man can be known as nothing else, then he may be known by his companions (10).

—SAKI FROM THE CHRONICLES OF CLOVIS

WE ARE HIS HANDS

We are physical beings created in His image—just look at our senses. We depend on them largely to experience our world. We long to hear God's voice, feel His arm around our shoulder, see the encouragement in His eyes, etc. Yet it seems we must largely go without because God is Spirit and appears to be physically inaccessible. So how do we reconcile the two?

He makes the whole body fit together perfectly. As each part does its own special work, it helps the other parts grow, so that the whole body is healthy and growing and full of love.

EPHESIANS 4:16 (NLT)

This scripture paints a picture of experiencing a powerful relationship with Jesus through fellow members of the body of Christ, regardless of age, race, socio-economic status or personality type. When we experience the fathering of God through each other, we actually connect with God on a physical or sensory level. Why would God create us as physical beings, if we were not supposed to connect with Him, at least in part, on some physical level? What we bring to each other is more than fellowship. We bring our Father's affirmation, wisdom, words, hugs, and even His voice. And other times, through our physical presence alone, we bring His fathering, even without saying a single word.

THE SACRED SILENCE

Sometimes we have no clue what to say to someone who is struggling. We're completely at a loss for words. We force ourselves to say something like "hang in there", but it doesn't offer much help to someone who really needs our support. Sometimes, all we can offer is our company, letting our physical presence communicate our care and solidarity. In the sacred silence, God fathers and heals us in profound ways.

I can remember a time when I told a brother my life story. I must have talked for at least an hour and a half without any interruption on his part. He just sat and listened. His nonverbal attentiveness gave me all the support I needed. At the end of the ninety minutes I felt I had been validated the whole time though he never spoke a single word. But it wasn't just my brother listening to my story, God was right there as well. What a powerful experience to have the eyes and ears of God tuned into your every word through a brother who is willing to walk alongside you.

CLIMBING NEW HEIGHTS

God chose to use the men at Base Camp (and one man in particular) to bring His fathering into my life. At times, it felt like open-heart surgery. If I had known how vulnerable I would become that weekend, I might not have even boarded the plane. But I did get on the plane. I made myself emotionally available (despite some initial protest), and I got my heart back, thankfully.

God didn't just want me to connect with a band of brothers. He wanted something more. God Himself wanted to connect with me *through* my brothers.

For when we are fathered and brothered we become courageous.

THE BROTHERING
INTERACTIVE STUDY QUESTIONS

1. When you think of the concept of God fathering through brothering, what comes to mind?

2. Describe a time when you experienced God's fathering through significant men in your life.

3. Describe a time when God brought his fathering through you to another brother.

4. What has gotten in the way of you receiving God's fathering in your life?

5. In what ways would you like to receive God's fathering through brothers?

6. In what ways do you feel drawn to bring God's fathering to others?

THE FATHERING

My son,

I am with you.

You are never alone.

I'm always with you.

I understand you need to see me with your eyes.

I understand you need to feel my hugs.

I understand you need to hear my voice.

I created you with all your senses so you could experience me
in a variety of ways.

I want you to trust me, son.

Trust that I will bring others to join you on your journey.

Let them bring my fathering to you.

Let their eyes be mine when they look at you with
compassion and love.

Let their listening ears be mine when they hear your story.

Let their voices give sound to my words of affirmation
and encouragement.

Let their hands and arms be mine when they give you a
handshake or a hug.

Experience my fathering through their brothering.

I love you.

Dad

A SON'S PRAYER

Dad,

You are everything to me.

There is no one I love more than you.

There is no one more important to me.

Father, help me to accept the brothers you bring into my life.

Help me to receive the fathering you have for me
through them.

Help me to remember that they are my brothers and only
you are my Father.

Thank you for my brothers.

Thank you for using their words to bring me your
encouragement, affirmation and even gentle rebuke.

Thank you for using their listening ears to show me
you hear me.

Thank you for using their arms to bring me your hugs, Dad.

Thank you for using their voices to give sound to your words.

You are the greatest Dad I could ever have.

I love you.

Amen

THE REDEMPTION

CHAPTER 12
THE COURAGEOUS MAN

Have I not commanded you? Be strong and of good courage;
do not be afraid, nor be dismayed, for the Lord your God is with
you wherever you go.

JOSHUA 1:9 (NKJV)

BEING a runner most of my life, I've always dreamed of qualifying for the Boston Marathon. The last time I attempted to qualify was rather demoralizing. Nearing the 20th mile, I started to wonder if I would even finish the dang thing. I knew I couldn't handle my current pace without encountering a lot more pain. When you redline your body for 20 miles, it feels like someone is shoving 18-inch needles up your legs starting from the bottom of your feet. Excruciating. So I did something I promised myself I would never do.

I quit.

If someone had asked me about it the next day, I probably would have gone into great detail about how ill-prepared I was. In hindsight, I was battling something more than just inadequate training. Something much more debilitating.

Fear.

And there it was again, that old familiar message. Only this time, it added a footnote to discourage any rebuttal.

You're on your own—you must rely on yourself for your strength. Oh, and by the way, your strength is running out.

THEY SHALL NOT BE WEARY

Now with God's help, I shall become myself (11).

—SOREN KIERKEGAARD

When we see our lives through the lens of God's fathering, it actually reframes our perspective on everything—even our past failures. As I began to write this chapter, I thought back on that race, only this time the picture was different. Very different.

Again, I'm running the marathon in an attempt to qualify for Boston. Like before, I get to mile 20, with pain searing through my entire body. But then the story takes on a whole new twist. Something catches my attention on the left side of the street. Someone is looking at me. It's God. He motions for me to come over to him. Puzzled, I slowly veer over to the side of the road where He stands. He bear hugs me, for starters, and then says something I can't quite make out, as the crowd noise drowns out His words. He speaks again, this time a bit louder.

"Son! Look into my eyes!"

As He says this, He gently pulls me close as He steadies me with His hands on my shoulders. We stand face to face. Then I noticed His eyes. His gaze pierces me like a laser beam boring into my very being.

Then something changes. Where there had once been pupils, tiny little mirrors now reflect an image of someone—someone I've never met before yet feel like I've known all my life. Father God was showing me the man He meant me to be. The man I truly was.

Then His voice boomed. "GO, son! GO!"

So I run with wild abandon, my feet barely touching the ground. With each step, strength and courage rise within me as I soar towards the finish line.

> *But those who wait on the Lord shall renew their strength; they shall mount up with wings like eagles, they shall run and not be weary, they shall walk and not faint.*
>
> ISAIAH 40:31(NKJV)

SEEING WITH MY FATHER'S EYES

A man of courage…

- Understands that admitting his weaknesses to God brings him strength, not shame or ridicule.
- Finds his identity in being God's son rather than what others think of him or his own performance.
- Faces his loneliness by deepening his connection with God and others instead of numbing it with addiction.
- Chooses to be more vulnerable with God and others instead of keeping himself isolated.
- Replaces his passivity with passion for the significant people in his life.

- Allows his own rescue to be a vehicle for God to rescue others.
- Depends on God as the source of his courage.

A man of courage is the man God meant for us to be. The man we truly are.

Say to those who are fearful-hearted, "Be strong, do not fear! Behold, your God will come with vengeance, with the recompense of God; He will come and save you." Then the eyes of the blind shall be opened, and the ears of the deaf shall be unstopped.

ISAIAH 35:4-5 (NKJV)

THE COURAGE TO REACH OUT

Experiencing the fathering of God through the brothering of men can inspire and embolden us to help others find their redemptive paths as well. Sometimes we reach into the flames and debris to rescue a desperate soul who reaches out to us from the rubble. Sometimes we walk alongside a brother who wrestles with his own demons and has yet to decide whether or not he's ready to take the next step. Whether in word or deed, we rely on our Father to lead us in this venture to help others.

And whatever you do in word or deed, do all in the name of the Lord Jesus, giving thanks to God the Father through Him.

COLOSSIANS 3:17 (NKJV)

I had coffee with an old friend the other day. He confessed his struggle with trusting God. He told me he wasn't sure if God was for him or against him because of all the misfortune in his life lately. I felt tempted to offer a quick response, but as I prayed quietly, it became clear what God wanted me to do—just listen. It was important that my friend felt understood and loved, instead of being treated like a problem that needed fixing. I hope my listening ears brought my friend a bit of God's fathering that afternoon.

It takes courage to follow God's leading when we live in a do-it-yourself world. Self-reliance can cause us to question the relevance and necessity of God's presence in our day-to-day lives. This is why we need our brothers to reinforce the reality of God's fathering for us. Otherwise, we slip back into passivity and isolation and, once again, travel the journey alone.

THE COURAGE TO BE FATHERED

For most of my Christian life, I treated God like a glorious vending machine. I thought if I just prayed the right prayer and had enough faith, God owed me an answer. Like someone who banged on the glass when the candy bar got stuck on the way down, I felt entitled to what I wanted. It was God's job to make me happy. What was ironic was that I didn't have a clue about what really satisfied my soul.

Just let me live my life, God—isolated, addicted, passive, full of shame and fatherless.

God wants to be so much more than a vending machine in our lives. It must sadden Him greatly when I cry out to Him only when I need something from Him. Like a teenage boy who approaches his father only when he needs more money, we often fail to realize we need God to be more than just our provider. We need Him to be our partner—walking the trail together fathering us along the way. Not so long ago, I prayed a prayer that absolutely terrified me at the time.

Father, do with me what you wish. As long as I have you, I have all I need.

But when I finished the prayer I felt peace—a peace that all my self-reliance had never provided. When we're willing to make ourselves vulnerable to God's fathering, He truly becomes the center of our lives—not out of obligation, but out of fondness for Him as our Father.

Becoming a man of courage does not mean we become fearless or invincible. It simply means we are willing to trust Him despite our fears and doubts. And we are willing to act on that trust as we embark on the great adventure with Father God.

A ship is safe in harbor, but that is not what ships are for (12).
—WILLIAM G.T. SHEDD

THE BROTHERING
INTERACTIVE STUDY QUESTIONS

1. What do you think of when you hear the word "courage"?

2. Describe a time when you felt courageous. What did it feel like? How did it impact your life? How did it impact those around you?

3. Now, envision yourself as a man of courage. What does that look like? What areas of your life are impacted?

4. When you think of the rubble in your life (addictions, passivity, isolation, fatherlessness, shame, etc.), where do you need courage the most?

5. Take time to pray and invite Father God into the areas of your life where you lack courage. Share what you notice with your brother(s).

6. Take time to pray and ask God to give you a picture of yourself as a man of courage. Does this picture differ from what you envisioned in question #3?

THE FATHERING

My son,
You have relied on your own strength for quite some
time now.
This has made you weak.
Fear and shame have convinced you to hide your
weaknesses from me.
This has prevented you from coming to me for courage
and strength.
You have believed the lie that you must do everything on
your own—out of your own strength.
Son, this has grieved me.
For so long, I have wanted you to come to me.
Come to me now, and let me father you.
Let me be your strength.
Let me give you the courage of a lion, my son.
Come to me, and look into my eyes.
And see yourself as I see you.
A man of courage.
This is the man I made you to be.
The man you truly are.

I love you, son.
Dad

A SON'S PRAYER

Dad,

I have relied on my own strength for too long.

I am so weak.

Fear and shame have told me to hide my weaknesses.

I believed them.

Forgive me.

I have also believed that I must do things on my own—
out of my own strength.

Forgive me for believing these lies, Father.

I come to you now. Please receive me.

You are my strength and courage.

I cannot manufacture those attributes on my own.

Help me to receive them now.

Show me who I am.

Let me see myself as you see me.

A man of courage.

I love you, Dad.

Amen

CONCLUSION

You'll use the old rubble of past lives to build anew, rebuild the foundations from out of your past. You'll be known as those who can fix anything, restore old ruins, rebuild and renovate, make the community livable again.

ISAIAH 58:12 (MSG)

W HEN we live fatherless and brotherless lives, a demolition occurs. Over time, the wrecking crew of isolation, addiction, passivity, and fear slowly demolishes our heart leaving us buried in the rubble. Oblivious to their destruction, we press on with our frantic lifestyles while keeping ourselves numbed, checked out and in survival mode. I certainly was not aware of the rubble in my life. I was convinced everything was fine. But it wasn't. Looking back, I was too distracted to see all the debris—too calloused to assess the damage. I had given up on my heart.

Thankfully, God doesn't give up on us.

FATHER ME

These two words can change everything: our marriages, our careers, our friendships, and our relationship with God. Everything.

More than my morality, integrity or nobility, God cares about my relationship with Him. It is paramount to everything else. This is where our rescue begins—with these two words— "father me".

A FEW GOOD MEN

God chooses to bring Himself to us in physical and tangible ways through the body of Christ. He knows we need Him to be touchable, audible, and visible. Often, He brings His fathering to us through the brothering of men. If we allow ourselves to be fathered in this way, it significantly deepens our relationship with God. We discover who we are as men because we know whose we are. We live as we were meant to live—with willingness, vulnerability, courage and passion.

So where do we go from here? Where do we find brothers to walk with along the journey? It may happen in a variety of ways. It may be a Rubble to Redemption Gathering or a group of guys at your local church. God will provide. He always does. The question remains—are you willing? Are you willing to humble yourself and become vulnerable with others?

My God shall supply all your need according to His riches in Christ Jesus.

PHILIPPIANS 4:19 (NKJV)

EPILOGUE

W ENDY picked me up at the airport that Sunday evening. Base Camp weekend was over, but my journey was just beginning. I got into the car and she could tell by the look in my eyes that something was different.

"So, how was your weekend?"

"You know. Same old, same old."

"Ah ha. Right." She stared at me not believing a word.

I leaned over and kissed her.

"Are you ok?"

"Do you recall the conversation we had about Base Camp a couple weeks ago?"

"Yeah…kind of."

"Remember when you said, 'This time might be different'."

"Yes."

"Well, it was definitely different."

"In a good way?"

"Yeah. In a very good way."

"Oh, good! I was praying it would be!" She smiled.

There it was again. That smile. That beautiful, amazing smile.

"Why are you looking at me like that?"

"I don't think I can stop. You're beautiful."

"Thanks." She said, looking a little embarrassed.

"You are, you know."

"Did someone kidnap my husband? Who is this man talking to me?" She said playfully.

"I guess it's time we both find out."

———————————— • ————————————

A PHONE CONVERSATION

Six months later…

"Hey, how you doin' this morning?" I looked down at my phone noticing the time. It was 8:07 AM.

"I'm good. Busy, but good." Ralph said with a chuckle.

"Busyness— it's a hard habit to break, brother."

"You got that right."

"Hey, you know, I don't think I've ever said it, but 'thanks'."

"For what?" Ralph asked.

"For reaching out to me that Saturday night at Base Camp."

"Well, He put you on my radar from the get-go that weekend."

"How so?"

"Well, it started during the first session on Thursday night. We were all asked to personalize a verse from the third chapter of Ecclesiastes and you said something like, 'A time to die' and something else I can't remember now."

"A time to resuscitate."

"Yeah. That was it. Man, you just seemed so willing to be vulnerable. That's what drew me in."

"I was not in good shape, that's for sure. Guess I felt I had nothing to lose."

"Well, He rescued both of us that weekend, brother." Ralph said.

"Amen to that."

"Man, we didn't have a clue, did we?"

"A clue about what?" I asked.

"About what God was going to do."

"Yeah, we had no idea we'd be starting this ministry or writing a book."

"Hard to believe this all happened in the last 6 months."

The conversation paused for moment, then a question popped into my mind.

"You think that Lone Ranger in us is dead, Ralph?"

Silence.

"Nope. There will always be the temptation to isolate. You can bet on that one." Ralph's voice took on a more somber tone. "This is why we make it a priority to stay in contact."

"We are a work in progress, aren't we?"

"Yes, but we are not alone."

As Ralph said those words, I thought of the men God had placed on my path over the past few months and the man I was now on the phone with who had become one of my best friends. God was fathering me through these men—revealing his faithfulness again and again.

For the first time in a long while, I wasn't so concerned with the future—just excited about the journey. I was on the trail with my Father riding shoulder to shoulder. And there was no other place I'd rather be.

ADDITIONAL INFORMATION

Please go to www.thomaspaulmills.com to contact me or leave a comment. I would love to hear how this book has impacted you!

TOM AND RALPH

You'll be like a well-watered garden, a gurgling spring that never runs dry. You'll use the old rubble of past lives to build anew, rebuild the foundations from out of your past. You'll be known as those who can fix anything, restore old ruins, rebuild and renovate, make the community livable again.

ISAIAH 58: 11-12 (MSG)

NOTES & REFERENCES

1. Tolkien, J.R.R. The Two Towers (The Lord of the Rings Trilogy Part 2) Houghton Mifflin Co. 2nd Rep Edition 1988.

2. Source: adapted from Lee, C & Glynn Owens, R (2002) The Psychology of Men's Health. Open University Press.

3. Retrieved from: http://www.brainyquote.com/quotes/quotes/m/mickeyrour 553319.html

4. The Christian Guest, Revised by N. Macleod, E MahlBokough & Co., London, 1858. Pg. 472.

5. Retrieved from: http://www.picturequotes.com/we-seldom-do-anything-to-the-best-of-our-ability-we-do-it-to-the-best-of-our-willingness-quote-4828

6. Retrieved from: http://www.goodreads.com/quotes/512034-to-share-your-weakness-is-to-make-yourself-vulnerable-to

7. The Monuments Men Motion Picture, 2014, Clooney, Milano: Twentieth century fox home entertainment.

8. Love in Action: Dad, Nearly 72, Races Nearly 1,100 Events with Disabled Son (Laura Coffee, Today News online, March 29, 2013).

9. Palmer, Parker J. A Hidden Wholeness: The Journey Toward an Undivided Life. 2009, San Francisco, CA, Jossey-Bass, pp. 59-60.

10. Munro, Hector Hugh. Pseud. Saki. The Chronicles of Clovis. 1911

11. Retrieved from: http://www.azquotes.com/quote/453264

12. Retrieved from: http//www.goodreads.com/quotes/1388-a-ship-is-safe-in-harbor-but-that-is-not-what

ABOUT THE AUTHOR

Thomas Paul Mills, MA, LP is an author, therapist and speaker. Licensed by the state of Minnesota as a psychologist, Tom has been providing therapy for individuals, couples, families and groups for the past 25 years. He has appeared on radio and television programs discussing anger management, men's issues and PTSD. Tom and his wife live in the Twin Cities. Some of his other passions include running, biking, enjoying the outdoors and composing music.

For more information, please visit **www.thomaspaulmills.com**.

Made in the USA
San Bernardino, CA
20 March 2017